W9-ADV-098

Reflections for Working Parents

The McGraw-Hill Reflections Series

Reflections for Working Women, CAROL TURKINGTON

Reflections for Managers, BRUCE HYLAND AND MERLE YOST

More Reflections for Managers, BRUCE HYLAND AND MERLE YOST

Forthcoming:

Reflections for the Workplace, BRUCE HYLAND AND MERLE YOST

Reflections for Working Parents

A Treasure Chest
of Truths
for Every
Working Parent

Carol A. Turkington

McGraw-Hill
New York San Francisco Washington, D.C. Auckland Bogotá
Caracas Lisbon London Madrid Mexico City Milan
Montreal New Delhi San Juan Singapore
Sydney Tokyo Toronto

Library of Congress Cataloging-in-Publication Data

Turkington, Carol.
Reflections for working parents / Carol A. Turkington.
p. cm. — (The McGraw-Hill reflections series)
ISBN 0-07-050514-4 (hardcover)
1. Working mothers. 2. Dual-career families. 3. Children of working parents. 4. Work and family. I. Title. II. Series.
HQ759.48.T94 1996
649'.1—dc20 96-34623
CIP

McGraw-Hill

*A Division of The **McGraw-Hill** Companies*

1 2 3 4 5 6 7 8 9 0 DOC/DOC 9 0 1 0 9 8 7 6

ISBN 0-07-050514-4

The sponsoring editor for this book was Susan Barry, the editing supervisor was Patricia V. Amoroso, and the production supervisor was Pamela A. Pelton. It was set in Palatino by Terry Leaden of McGraw-Hill's Professional Book Group composition unit.

Printed and bound by R. R. Donnelley & Sons Company.

This book is printed on recycled, acid-free paper containing a minimum of 50% recycled, de-inked fiber.

For Our Daughter,
Kara Aislinn Kennedy,
with Love

Contents

The Day to Day

Partner Techniques

Working at Home

Single Parents

Introduction

The day stands isolated in my memory: The new baby was screaming with colic. Mounds of laundry were piled around the room, dirty dishes filled the sink, and the vacuum cleaner didn't work. Papers were strewn around my home office, I had two deadlines to meet that day, and I hadn't slept more than a few hours a night in 3 weeks.

I was a working mom, and at that moment I hated it. What had seemed to be an idyllic compromise—writing at home while gently rocking my sweetly sleeping infant—was in fact impossible. I had no time for me, no time to work, and no time to spend with my baby. I thought longingly of how things were when I was little, back in the halcyon 1950s when my mom stayed home and baked cookies while my dad went out and earned a living. Life seemed blissful, uncomplicated, and secure back then. But the fathers who marched out the door each morning on the way to work were distant and uninvolved in their children's lives. My own father never changed a diaper, washed a dish, or baked a potato. Mothers were left at home holding pearls and a vacuum cleaner, with no options and no dreams.

For many women of the 1950s, it was a kind of safety born of imprisonment.

In the ensuing 40 years, the worlds of "work" and "home" have collided, with predictable results. Today many men are actively involved in raising their children, and many women are able to pursue careers. In fact, an increasingly insecure economy has made it almost imperative that both parents work outside the home in order to provide basic necessities for their families.

Unfortunately, corporate America has not kept pace with these changes. Company rules and practices, created in the day when men went to work and their wives stayed home, remain unchanged—in spite of the fact that fewer than 7 percent of American families fit that model today. Many employers have been even slower to embrace the idea of family-friendly employment practices when they have to promote the idea of women in the work place. As a result, working parents struggle to findways to balance work and family in the face of unbending employers and unrelenting responsibility.

I learned a great deal about the world of working parents in the course of writing this book. Not the least of what I learned was a profound respect for the many men and women in America who struggle daily with overwhelming guilt and responsibility. Every working parent I interviewed spoke in anguished terms of the dilemma: They don't have enough time with their kids. They can't take off from work when a child is sick. They feel guilty for putting their children in day care.

It's the unbearable stress of trying to juggle work, home, and family in the 1990s.

It's a scenario with which I'm very familiar, since I continued my writing career at home while raising our daughter. People who have never tried this have a romantic idea of what it's like to combine work, home, and child care. I'm here to tell you it was no day at the beach. My husband made equal sacrifices. When I was struggling at home during Kara's first 5 years, Michael accepted a significant cut in salary to work 4-day weeks, allowing me one full day on Fridays when I knew I could schedule trips to New York, conduct interviews, and concentrate on all-day writing marathons. We'd each take a weekend day to work on projects, and we shared late-night child-care duty. We also took turns sleeping in, one morning each on the weekend. It wasn't easy, yet our life was a breeze compared with that of moms and dads who must work outside the home. Single working parents have the most difficult time of all.

Still, while writing this book, I discovered the picture isn't all bleak. There are pockets of enlightenment among smaller companies whose leaders recognize that encouraging flexibility among employees with children is good business. These employers have realized that family-friendly policies will attract and hold good employees. They understand that those who aren't overly stressed by family concerns are more productive and absent less often.

Gradually, out of the crucible of emotion has come the realization that it's just not possible to be perfect at home and at work, and that no one should expect it of any of us. It is simply unrealistic and unfair for employers to expect their workers to act as if their families don't exist.

We must stop comparing ourselves as working parents to unreachable ideals. We have to learn to set priorities, to ask for help. There's no way we can come home from a stressful job and cook dinner, clean house, feed the pets, play with the children, and relate to our partner, all with perfect equanimity during that brief window between 6:00 and 9:00 P.M.

What I discovered while writing this book is that working parents have learned to think creatively in solving many of their most painful dilemmas. Nowhere is this more evident than on computer on-line services such as the Internet: Parenting message boards function as a sort of global back fence where moms and dads meet to exchange ideas and vent frustration. I was particularly impressed by the offers of real support and friendship on-line.

"I'm sorry to hear how rough you have it," parents say to one another. "Here's how I coped with that situation..."

For this book I interviewed men and women from around the country, from all walks of life. I asked them: How do you cope? What are your frustrations, your problems, and your joys about being working parents? Together, we shared our experiences, our methods, our pain, and our triumph.

I was particularly impressed by the dedicated dads, who spoke honestly of the problems and trials of those actively seeking to be involved in raising their children as their own fathers never were.

What I found most heartening is that despite all the problems, more and more working parents—moms and dads alike—actively embrace both the frustration and the joy that comes from contributing not just financially, but emotionally, to their children's lives.

I wrote this book for them.

Carol A. Turkington

...The most important job in the world is the making of another human being, one to whom we have given roots and wings.

—Ashley Montagu

Reflections for Working Parents

And Baby Makes Three

EMPHASIZE COMMITMENT

When discussing family leave, open your negotiations by emphasizing your commitment and value to the company.

In More Depth

When you're approaching your boss with the idea that you want to take some time off after the baby, realize that his or her first concern is probably going to be for the company. Bosses don't get to be bosses by forgetting the bottom line, and there may well be some concern about how dedicated or committed you will be if you're planning on jumping ship—even if you say it's only temporary.

Indeed, some bosses may have experience with employees who swore they would come back, only to misjudge the strength of their desire to stay at home with the baby. No matter how much you deny this possibility, odds are it's going to be flitting through your boss's mind and may well underlie all the negotiations.

The more you can emphasize your commitment and value to the company—provided this is how you really feel—the more likely that your boss will at least be willing to consider your proposal.

Mom's Point of View

When Harriet, an editor with a small publishing firm, realized she wanted to try job sharing with another editor, she wasn't at all sure that her bosses would go for the plan. It had never been done before.

She was not entirely convinced that such a radical step—which would create a precedent—would be a popular move.

Before approaching her bosses, Harriet and the other woman spent several months hammering out a proposal in their spare time. They both emphasized their mutual commitment to the company and their willingness to make this unique arrangement work. Step by step, they ticked off reasons the proposal not only would work, but would actually benefit the company.

"They took 2 weeks to review our proposal, and then they gave us a counterproposal," Harriet recalled. A key point was that Harriet and the other editor would begin the situation on a trial basis for 3 months, and if either the women or their bosses had a problem, the arrangement would not continue.

After 3 months, Harriet and her coeditor were thrilled with the system and their bosses admitted they had experienced absolutely no problems. "We were willing to give whatever we needed to keep going," Harriet says. "The key was in presenting the proposal in their terms, not in ours. We emphasized what *they* would be getting out of the arrangement, and how committed we were to the company and to making this proposal work."

Dad's Point of View

Trevin is a midlevel manager whose wife recently became pregnant with their first child. He decided that he wanted to take family leave, but he was nervous about how to approach his boss. "We don't really have a family-friendly company," he says, "and while I know the law requires the company to offer leave, there are some unspoken rules around the office. Most men don't avail themselves of the opportunity, just like no one actually says you're expected to work late, but everyone does it."

What Trevin says is true. There is often a big difference between formal policy and the unwritten company "rules." Even in those companies that openly encourage paternity leave, many men don't take it because of worries over their career.

Trevin agonized over his decision, since he very much wanted to be home with the baby but didn't want to jeopardize his career. Eventually his wife convinced him that if the company was so unpleasant as to deny him a chance to be with his own child, perhaps it was not the sort of company he would be happy working for.

He decided to open negotiations by emphasizing his commitment to the job and explaining how he wanted to continue working for the company after the birth. He then explained how his duties could be handled in his absence, carefully going over his responsibilities and discussing which employees could handle the job. He offered to train the people who would be filling in for him.

All was going well until the boss countered Trevin's offer of a 6-month leave with a suggestion of a 3-month hiatus. But because Trevin had prepared himself, he unveiled his backup position: He offered to return sooner on a part-time basis, or suggested that he could work from home. His boss approved the part-time approach, and they were both satisfied. By offering a solution, not an ultimatum, Trevin had achieved his goals with a minimum of unpleasantness.

For Reflection

Put yourself in your boss's shoes for a moment, and imagine how you would feel when an employee comes in with a request for family leave. What would be your concerns?

Before you approach your boss, write down all the points you intend to bring up. Make sure you stress commitment right up front.

What is the least amount of family leave with which you could be comfortable? Are you prepared to accept the fact that you may not be granted the leave you want?

CHANGE IS EVOLUTIONARY

No matter what the popular press says, change—especially in the workplace—takes time. This is true for moms who want to combine work and home, and it's especially true for dads who want to put their family first.

In More Depth

American society today certainly offers more options and more flexible arrangements for those families who need to combine work and parenting. But while the picture is changing, it's still far from perfect. Many women still find they are penalized for wanting to stay home with their babies. Men encounter confusion and condescension on the job when they dare to voice their wish to pay less attention to the job and more attention to their families.

What makes it even more difficult is that, before birth, it's extremely hard to imagine how strong the parent-child bond can be. Many parents who assure employers they will return soon after the baby comes find that it is nearly impossible to do so.

Mom's Point of View

Susan was the highest-ranking woman executive at her bank when she became pregnant and approached her bosses about instituting some sort of flexible scheduling so that she could combine motherhood with work. To her surprise, she was met with an iron wall of resistance.

While women in less demanding positions were beginning to discreetly arrange various flextime schedules, no one in upper-level management had dared to approach the boss with such a request.

"I was told I was not allowed to try working on a flextime schedule," Susan recalls. "My superiors were all men, and their wives had stayed at home to raise the children. They had no idea what I was talking about."

When the bank absolutely refused to listen to her proposals, Susan handed in her resignation and went into business for herself instead as a financial consultant. Now she has the flexibility she needs and the freedom she craves to combine both her job and her family.

While "family leave" today is mandatory by law, very few firms have made a real effort to give employees who are raising a family other options: family-friendly scheduling, flextime, job sharing, or other innovative compromises. It's important to be aware that some firms are more willing to explore options than others. Be prepared with a backup plan if your firm isn't willing to work with you.

Dad's Point of View

When Fred and Joan had their first child, it made more sense for Joan to keep working at her job as an attorney at a prestigious firm, so Fred took a 6-month family leave from his marketing firm. "At first, my colleagues wished me well and told me they wished they could do the same thing," he recalls. But over time, Fred began to notice that the attitudes of the other men changed. They began to take over his accounts and shut him out from key decisions. When he would call the office to check in, he felt that the others treated him with condescension and a lack of respect. "No matter what they said," Fred reported, "deep down inside they seemed to lose respect for me as a businessman. I think they saw me as a wimp."

What was even more surprising to Fred was that when talking

about his situation to others, he would find himself hinting that he was working from home instead of "sitting around and taking care of the baby." While Fred had thought he was completely untraditional and forward-thinking, he was dismayed to see the attitude of his peers—and his own response to their actions. As they treated him with increasing contempt, he began to feel ashamed of his "house husband" role.

What Fred found out was that it can be painful to be in the forefront of social change. Try to keep in mind that you're doing what you think best for your family. Your sacrifices today will make it that much easier for your sons and daughters as they begin to juggle the twin roles of worker and parent.

For Reflection

Understand that it may not be easy to convince your employer to try an alternative work schedule. Can you live with the refusal?

You may be breaking new ground when you come up with alternative work options. How can you present your proposal so that it sounds right not just for you, but for the company?

Look around you at people you know who have developed innovative job management strategies. What can you learn from them?

PLAN YOUR LEAVE

When you are ready to approach your boss about family leave, take time to think about what you're asking for and what you're willing to give back to the company.

In More Depth

While you can't pinpoint when your baby will arrive, you do have control over how you negotiate your family leave to prepare for the baby's arrival. Before you actually present your boss with a plan, make sure you know what you and your partner want and need. How much time will you require, and how do you want to come back to work—gradually or all at once? What child-care options do you have? Is there a possibility for working out some sort of flexible work arrangements?

You'll also need to know exactly what benefits your company offers—the availability of paid and unpaid leave, whether health insurance continues during your time off, whether your disability coverage extends to pregnancy and childbirth.

By thinking through all the possibilities—what your company offers and what you think you'll need—you'll be in a better position to negotiate with your boss.

Mom's Point of View

The second in command at a medium-size business, Lorna was contemplating her upcoming pregnancy and trying to steel herself to ask for some extra time off. She stewed about the problem for weeks, putting off the showdown with her boss time and again. She was terrified she would be told she could have no extra time beyond the 6 weeks her company usually offered.

"You can't just burst into his office and ask for time off," her sister counseled. "Take some time to put together a plan for your leave, and make sure to include some things that show you're willing to negotiate."

Deciding that her sister was right and it couldn't hurt to ask, Lorna went in to see her boss and presented a careful plan in which she would agree to stay on the job until the very end if he would allow her 3 weeks after the baby arrived with no interruptions. After that, she volunteered to be available by phone and fax for emergencies for the remainder of her leave.

To her surprise, her boss was impressed with her professional attitude and willingness to compromise, and offered her 5 months of paid maternity leave if she would keep her end of the bargain.

"Have a game plan," she advises, "and think about the questions that may come up. That about what you can give in return, and you may be pleasantly surprised."

Dad's Point of View

Jim is an Internet specialist at his big-city nonprofit association who was able to take advantage of his firm's paternity leave after his daughter's birth. Before he left, he presented his plan for taking more time after his paternity leave was up: He would use his disability insurance and accumulated leave to work part time for the first 6 months. This proposal was accepted.

"My company is a pretty supportive environment and my boss was very helpful. My colleagues decided to pitch in and take up the slack rather than hiring someone else to do my job, and you can't ask for more support than that." When Jim came back part time, he found it was not an easy task. "It's hard to get up to speed and stay focused, because there's not always a tomorrow when you can polish it off." Jim says he appreciated being able to take paternity leave, and that he treasured time he could be there at home to help out and spend time with his daughter."

For Reflection

Think of three concessions you could offer your boss in return for an extended leave.

How might presenting a logical, balanced plan improve your chances of getting the leave you're hoping for?

Have you addressed all your boss's potential concerns in your proposal for leave?

DON'T FEEL GUILTY

It's often hard to imagine your feelings after your baby arrives. If your attitude does change about how you look at your job, accept this as natural, and act accordingly.

In More Depth

Many new mothers and fathers confidently expect they'll be ready to go right back to work within weeks after their baby's birth. It can be a shock (especially to a woman who is adamant about the value of day care) when some parents fall so completely in love with their infant that they have no desire to return to work.

Others have the opposite reaction. They feel guilty because they find the nonstop baby care taxing, and they long to return to the stimulation of the workplace. It's important to realize that both extremes are completely normal. You're not less of an adult if you long to stay home with your child, and you're not less of a parent if you yearn for the stimulation of the job. The important thing is to *accept* your feelings and go on from there.

Mom's Point of View

Jane is a successful lawyer who edits a legal magazine and has always been an achiever with high standards. She and her husband had waited a long time before having their first child, and Jane had expected that she would be more than ready to return to her office. She was totally unprepared for her reluctance to do so.

"I didn't think I would have such a strong pull to be at home with our daughter, to be committed to her in this way," Jane says. "I don't think I could have imagined her before she was in my life. Now that she's here, it seems so right to have one of us home with her for a big chunk of time." Jane is fortunate to have found another woman to share her job, and the two have hammered out a successful partnership.

"Motherhood keeps tugging at me," Jane says, "and more and more voices in my head are saying this is what I need to be doing."

Dad's Point of View

James feels guilty for slightly different reasons. He misses his daughter while he's at work, since he gets to see her only about 2 hours a day. His wife has been able to continue her career as a beauty products consultant from her home office. But the stress of trying to manage the home, continue her job, and take care of their daughter makes her tired, edgy, and frustrated much of the time.

"I come home after being at work all day, and I feel guilty," James says. "My wife has to contend with so much and I feel like no matter what I do, it's not enough." Inevitably, child care and household duties fall to the one who is at home every day to take care of them.

"I tried to make things better by coming home every day for lunch," he says, "but then I realized I was just leaving my wife with more dirty dishes to wash, and I didn't have time to take care of them before I had to leave again for work."

He copes with his guilty feelings as best he can by helping out in the evenings and spending time on the weekends scrubbing floors and vacuuming. "My wife wanted to hire someone to clean the house and

I was afraid we couldn't afford it," he said, "but then I realized that this might be one way to equalize the household chores a bit."

For Reflection

How many times in the past week did you feel guilty for not doing something you felt you "should" have done?

Think back on how your own parents handled jobs and parenthood. How different is your way from their way?

What do you want your child to remember about his or her childhood? Are those thoughts realistic?

THINK IT THROUGH

Whatever your plans are for working after the baby comes, take time to fully contemplate what sorts of accommodations you will make and communicate fully with your partner about feelings and expectations.

In More Depth

It's hard to imagine what that first child will do to your life, how it will change your feelings and outlook. Many working parents—especially those who are heavily invested in their careers—are astounded at the way their opinions about their life and work choices alter once the baby comes.

At the same time, studies have shown that sometimes this change in feelings is more profound for women than for men. When this happens in marriages where both partners had been heavily invested in dual-career marriages, men sometimes resent their wives' change in attitude. This is especially true for men and women whose social life revolved around their careers. It also appears that to a far greater degree, men don't experience the same sense of isolation and loss of control as their wives. The studies suggest this may be because often men's lives remain basically the same after the birth, with no conflict between work and child care.

Mom's Point of View

Many career women, especially those who have waited to have a child, say they never realized what a pull motherhood would exert.

Many of these mothers say they automatically assumed they'd be happy to go back to work and get into the routine after the birth—until the baby came.

"I fell in love," says Kira, a corporate attorney. "I worked so hard to achieve my present position. I never believed that I would want to turn my back on my job for an instant. Unfortunately, for that reason I hadn't asked for much leave."

When she approached the partners for more time, they grudgingly agreed to a few more weeks, but they were not pleased. "I'm not sure they would have given me more time up front, but it would probably have been better if I had arranged things that way," she says. "They don't like to be surprised, and it was harder for them to find someone to take over my work."

Dad's Point of View

There was absolutely no way that Dan could have prepared himself for the way he felt about his new baby daughter. A computer analyst, he had heard the stories about people "falling in love" with their child, but he was sure it would be different for him.

"I'm basically a fairly restrained guy," he said, "and I couldn't imagine gushing over a baby—even my own. I thought that was something women did."

The day his daughter was born changed his mind and his life. "I couldn't stop looking at her. I couldn't stop playing with her," he said. "She was all I thought about. The idea of actually going to work and leaving her was absolutely impossible." He had accepted his firm's 3-month family leave as a way of helping his wife, but now he was glad that he had the time himself to spend with his baby. "If they hadn't given me that leave, I would probably have asked for only a week," he says. "I just didn't realize what it would mean to be a father."

For Reflection

How clearly have you thought about how much time you want to take after the baby is born?

If you change your mind about how soon you want to go back to work, will you be able to take more time if you need it?

Consider adding an extra 3 months to the time you originally planned to take. Then if you want to come back early, you'll be able to—but if you don't, you'll have already planned for it.

FIND A JOB-SHARE PARTNER

If you have the sort of job that can be split up, why not try to find someone to share the work? This way, everyone wins

In More Depth

While job sharing is still a fairly new idea in the workplace, it's becoming more popular as a way of balancing career and child care. Of course, some jobs may be simpler to share than others: A clerical position that requires someone to answer the phones all day is a fairly simple one to share. But even management and upper-level positions can be shared if it's possible to split the job's functions.

One editor managed to split her job by dividing the manuscripts she handled with a partner, with each woman spending two and a half days in the office. One day a week, their schedules overlapped so they could stay in contact with what needed to be done.

Breaking new ground with such job-share arrangements does require you to be flexible, such as agreeing to attend important meetings on an "off" day or take phone calls at home when necessary.

Mom's Point of View

Miranda is an office manager for a large insurance company who first thought about job sharing when her 12-month-old son was born. She'd heard about the possibility from a friend of hers who had been successfully sharing her job for some time.

"The problem was, I didn't know how to go about finding someone to share with," Miranda says. "I figured I'd just go to my boss and get him to help me find a job-share partner." It wasn't a successful ploy. Her boss told her adamantly that the job was a full-time position for one person, and if she didn't like it he could find someone to take over who didn't have kids at home. What Miranda hadn't realized is that the responsibility of finding a job-sharing partner was hers, not her boss's. She left the job soon afterward, and applied for a similar job with a competitor across town.

She had not forgotten her dream of job sharing, but she had learned her lesson. Her friend Alison had referred her to another woman who was looking for a job-share partner, and the two hit it off immediately. When Alison went back for her second interview with the insurance company, she presented her plan to share the job. The boss was impressed with the businesslike approach and her well-thought-out plan, called the second woman in for an interview, and hired them both.

Dad's Point of View

Rob had been a graphic artist for many years and enjoyed his job as layout designer for a large nonprofit organization. But after he and his wife had their second child, he realized he really wanted more time at home with the baby. Because his job was fairly straightforward, he was able to present a plan to the editors whereby he and another artist would share the layout chores. One month, Rob would design the layout and the other artist would carry out the plans; the next month, they would reverse their roles.

Far from feeling competitive, the two artists enjoyed working together and found that their styles complemented each other. "And this way, I can spend more time at home with the kids without worrying about losing the job," Rob says.

For Reflection

If you've found a prospective job-sharing partner, do you have the same work philosophy? Do you have complementary skills and experience?

Can you work with someone else on a project without being overly competitive?

Do you you feel like you're always the leader with the best ideas?

On the Job

TIME FOR A NEW JOB?

If you've decided your present position is just too rigid, it may be time to look for a more family-friendly, flexible position.

In More Depth

While discussion of family-friendly jobs sounds wonderful on paper, in reality far too many American companies have not yet realized that for most of their employees, families do come first. If you work for inflexible employers who just can't see it your way, you may someday come to a point where the happiness of your family requires you to find another job.

More and more often men and women alike are turning away from employers who won't consider day-care options, flexible scheduling, altered workweeks, job sharing, or other innovative compromises. Other companies set up systems that seem helpful but that really don't solve employees' problems. For example, one large corporation receives lots of publicity for its subsidized on-site day care. But as one woman discovered, only a small minority of the company's employees could take advantage of the program. She signed up for the on-site care when she was 3 months pregnant; her child is now 4 years old and a vacancy still hasn't become available. What's worse, no subsidies are given to employees who must place their children elsewhere.

Mom's Point of View

For some working moms, employee inflexibility is the impetus behind finding parent-friendly work. Sybil is a county employee who juggles a hectic work schedule and a long commute and worries about what to do with her young daughter when her preschool closes for the summer. "I work for a bureaucracy that doesn't believe in flextime and won't consider it," she says. "It's the position of the court administrator for our department that our schedules are inflexible. Basically, he was saying that it didn't matter what the employees need—we are here to serve the public." But in Sybil's department, "Our public is people on parole; in fact it would suit their purposes much better if we did have flextime, because they could come in before work or after work to meet with the parole officers."

Because her employers won't deviate from their position, Sybil has come to the conclusion that she needs to find a different job. For the past 2 years she's been going to graduate school at night, working toward certification to teach. Trying to combine school, job, and child care adds a tremendous burden to her already tight schedule, but Sybil believes it's the only choice she has. "Teaching is the only job I'm aware of in this town that will allow me the time I'd like to have to be with our daughter during the summer and during the school year."

Dad's Point of View

When Sam's auto parts job ended with the bankruptcy of the business, he quickly found a new position at another dealership in the next county. At first it seemed like an ideal switch, since his benefits were much better and his salary almost doubled. But these perks came at a high cost.

Because the dealership was much farther away, he was on the road a full 2 hours more per day. He and his wife had recently had their first child, and Sam's long commute was a real hardship for the couple.

To make matters worse, the policy at the new shop required employees to work one or two Saturdays a month and an extra evening once a week. Sam initially took the job because it was the only opening he could find, but the burden of the extra commute and the inflexibility of the owners caused problems at home. Most of the other employees didn't have children. "There was kind of a macho atmosphere and nobody could understand my point," he says. "I felt like I never saw my family. At some point you have to ask yourself what you're working for. Are a few more dollars a week really worth missing my daughter's early years?" Sam says he was starting to feel like a stranger in his own home.

Eventually, the stress of the commute outweighed the better salary and benefits. Sam found a job within 15 minutes of home at a small private shop. It paid less money and the benefits were almost nonexistent, but Sam could come home for lunch every day and was not required to work any extra hours. Even better, this company was family-friendly and small enough so that he was always able to get away for school outings and other important family business. "All the money in the world won't make up for the fact that I wasn't around to watch my baby grow," he says. "I'd quit any job that interfered with that."

For Reflection

Are your employers supportive of your family's needs? Are they willing to listen to your concerns?

It's entirely possible that if your employer hasn't already set up flexible systems, your suggestions will be met with disapproval or hostility. Are you prepared to be turned down when you make a proposal or alternate scheduling?

When looking for a new job, find out the company's attitude toward family responsibilities. Make sure the company's outlook matches your own feelings or there could be problems later on.

THINK POSITIVE

Try to focus not on what you're missing by being at work, but on what you're able to give to the family because you are: money, self-respect, outside interests.

In More Depth

One of the hardest things for parents who work full time is handling the guilt and disappointment of not "being there" every moment for their children. The feelings can be intense for both partners, although they may occur for slightly different reasons. Many women who feel subtle yet intense pressure from society to be at home for their children feel unbearable guilt when they must leave the youngsters in day care all day in order to work. And while husbands have long borne the mantle of "provider," many still feel disappointment at missing special moments with their children.

Since in many cases parents work because they *must,* quitting to stay at home with the kids may not be an option. If this is the case, feeling guilty, resentful, or disappointed isn't going to help anyone. The most recent studies have shown that children whose parents love them do not suffer from being placed in good day-care situations. Try to concentrate not on what you're missing, but on the benefits that your job can provide.

Chances are your salary is providing necessities and benefits that will give your child a better life. Many parents say they are happier, better adjusted people because of maintaining a career, which in turn benefits their youngsters.

Mom's Point of View

Mariellen, a mother of three children ages 6, 4, and 3, has to work full-time because of financial problems. Because she makes more money than her partner, she cannot quit or even go part-time. "I have never come to terms with the guilt I feel every day when I have to go to work," she says. She struggles with those feelings every day.

What has made her feel better is knowing that her children are happy in day care and that they are outgoing, friendly youngsters at ease in social situations because of their daily encounters with others. Moreover, she was comforted by the fact that, according to pediatrician T. Berry Brazelton, most children practice new skills long before a parent actually sees them do it. "There was no reason for me to be upset at missing my child's first step," she says, "since it was not likely that the day-care giver was actually seeing the very real first step anyway." What is now important to Mariellen is that the first time *she* sees her child's skill is still a "first" with her, and that's what really matters.

Dad's Point of View

Tim is an elementary school teacher who says that leaving his son behind in day care is hard to do. "I would stay at home in a minute if we didn't need my salary, or if there was something I could do at home," he says. But while it pains him to have to leave for work every day before his son is up, and come home right before the child's bedtime, he says he is comforted because of the time he does have to spend with the family on the weekends, when the money he brings home can pay for trips to the beach, visits to the theater, and educational toys.

"My own father abandoned my mom when I was 6," he says, "so I am willing to make sacrifices like going to work because I know that I'm here for the important stuff, the way my father never was."

For Reflection

Think back over the past month. How many times did you do something just for fun?

Make a list of the times when you feel unhappy about working. Now make a list of all the things your salary can provide for your family that you couldn't otherwise afford.

Are you concerned about your kids in day care because of what others will think or because they are truly unhappy?

TAKE YOUR CHILD TO WORK

While taking a child to work is not an option for everyone, those parents who can do so find it to be a successful solution in a pinch.

In More Depth

Back in April 1993, the Ms. Foundation introduced the idea of a "Take Your Daughters to Work" day as a method to expose young girls to the world of work. But many parents don't wait for April to take their kids to the job, and they don't limit it to girls.

Your job may seem humdrum to you, but odds are your kids will find it fascinating: They like seeing what you do every day, eating in the cafeteria, playing with supplies.

If it's not feasible occasionally to bring your kids to work with you during the day, you could try bringing them to work on a weekend or after hours on a week night. Those who work in places such as dairy farms, fire stations, libraries, and grocery stores can sometimes arrange tours so your child's whole class can visit.

The important thing is to introduce your child to the place where you spend much of your day, so that he or she will come to understand a little more of why you must sometimes sacrifice time at home to time at work.

Mom's Point of View

Bonnie is a full-time freelance writer who maintains an office in the city near where her kindergartner Shelby goes to school. Although

Bonnie is able to work regular hours, she must still leave her office at 2:30 P.M. to pick up her daughter, often leaving important work unfinished.

"On days when I'm on a serious deadline, I'll bring my daughter back with me to the office," she says. "I try to make this a special time so she'll look forward to it, and so far it's worked."

Each time she brings her daughter to work, Bonnie stops off at the coffee shop next door and buys cocoa with whipped cream to take along to the office. Bonnie keeps special coloring books and crayons on a shelf for her daughter, and gives her little "jobs" to do on the Xerox machine.

"So far, coming to the office is fun for her. She also likes to go with my husband to his auto shop on Saturdays when it's quiet. She helps operate the lift, plays with the tires, and does odd jobs around the shop."

Dad's Point of View

Bart is a full-time architect who longs to spend more time with his daughter, but who must work for financial reasons. As a compromise, he sometimes brings her to work on days when babysitters fall through or he wants to spend some extra time with his child.

"The first thing I did was to let her pick out some toys for herself that would remain under my drafting table at the office," Bart says. These were her "office toys" that she was allowed to play with only in the office. Bart set up a space for her to "work," stamping envelopes and punching holes.

"It worked out well, and the more often she was there, the calmer she got."

For Reflection

Do you ever talk about work situations with your children in a way that helps the kids understand what you do and why?

Do you think your kids understand what you really do all day? If you ask, you may be surprised at their responses.

Before you bring your children to work, make a list of possible things with which they can amuse themselves. Bring a few toys along if you fear they might get bored before you need to leave.

ASK FOR WHAT YOU WANT

If your situation seems less than ideal, don't wait for someone to come and rescue you. Look around and create for yourself the situation you need.

In More Depth

Sometimes it seems as if we just don't have any options, especially if we've been in the same job for a long period of time. We fall into ruts. We tend to see only the part of the path that is right in front of us.

If you're having trouble juggling family and job responsibilities, it may help to try to think about things a bit differently. It's a sure bet that the job won't change unless *you* change it—and it's often surprising how willing an employer can be to accept change rather than lose a valued employee.

Mom's Point of View

Peggy was a software engineer for the U.S. Army and struggled with lots of stress, loads of travel, and incredibly long hours. She was trying to raise her child and keep up with her job, but it looked like a losing battle. She knew that the next year would be even worse.

"One of our contractors was always talking about how overworked he was, and how he wished he could find someone who enjoyed technical writing." As it happened, Peggy's favorite part of her job was writing. What could she lose?

She called the contractor and asked for a job—provided she could work primarily at home, and wouldn't have to travel.

"He accepted my offer, and here I am," she says today. "I've been working at home and loving every minute of it." Her hours are flexible, so she can finally volunteer at her son's school and go on field trips without begging for permission from her boss. She doesn't go into a frenzy of "should I stay or go" when her son is sick, and she doesn't have to worry about finding backup care when the day-care worker goes on vacation.

"Mom is happier, and everyone else is too," she reports.

Dad's Point of View

Dave's job as an automotive technician at a busy foreign car shop left him little time to see his 4-year-old daughter. His company also required him to work one evening a week, which cut into his family time even more. His wife worked at home but struggled with combining family and career responsibilities, and Dave knew she was often snowed under with work.

"It seemed so unfair," he recalled, "to have her working all those hours and trying to take care of our daughter too. I could see it was making her irritable, and I wasn't getting to see enough of our daughter."

Figuring he would have nothing to lose, he went to the shop owner and asked if he could work a 4-day week and opt out of the evening schedule. The boss could see that Dave was a solid employee who was trying to come up with a plan to help his family as well, and he didn't want to lose him.

"To my surprise, they agreed to my plan. I was able to work just 4 days a week for 2 years, until our daughter was old enough for kindergarten. If I hadn't asked, all that time would have been lost to me."

For Reflection

What would you like to change about your job that would enhance your family life?

Can you list three ways to change your present job that would make it easier for you to fulfill parenting responsibilities?

What's the worst thing that could happen if you asked your boss for a change in your job?

KIDS AND CONFERENCES DO MIX

Consider bringing your kids if you must attend a conference; it can be a fun way to combine job and home life.

In More Depth

Today's working parents find that it's possible to take a baby or an older child to a working conference and not destroy their career—but it requires lots of forethought and planning.

Many large professional conferences these days offer day-care services if you register in advance. And if you bring along a spouse, you may find that conferences can be interesting ways to spend some time together as a family as well as get some work done.

Still, it's not always easy to conduct yourself in a professional setting and project a professional image while caring for a baby or young child in a new environment. This is where thinking ahead and planning come in handy; not many hotels or college bathrooms have changing tables, for example. But with some forethought, many parents today find that bringing kids along to conferences not only is possible, but is a lot more fun than eating alone in a strange town.

Mom's Point of View

Dana is an investment counselor who was happy to discover that her husband would be allowed to attend her conference for free in order to care for their child. "The conference administrators reasoned that it was sort of like having a person push a wheelchair," she says. "After all, my husband wasn't interested in the conference information—he just wanted to help me."

Dana's husband followed her around, carrying the baby in a Snugglee. Dana notes that her best decision was to stay at the hotel where the conference took place, since she always needed a place to nurse. "And don't worry if you miss a talk or two," she says. "Be easy on yourself."

Dad's Point of View

Many times conference planners will bend over backward to ease the way for parents who must bring their youngsters along for the ride. Some allow parents to have young children at meals for free. Others provide access for an accompanying spouse.

Sam is an insurance adjuster who accompanied his wife on an important conference, together with their 9-month-old son. During the day, Sam and the baby toured the city and took in the sights, thoroughly enjoying themselves. "I took time to see things I never would have bothered with otherwise," he said. He was a little concerned at first about feeling out of place as a sort of "Mr. Mom," and wondered privately how the other men at the conference would perceive him. He found out he worried needlessly.

"A lot of the men at the conference had young children at home, and one famous researcher whipped out his baby's pictures to show me," Sam said. "We're all human, after all."

For Reflection

Think back over your last convention. Would your kids have enjoyed going along?

Are you able to juggle your work and parenting roles easily, moving from one to the other without a problem?

How many times in the last year were you forced to travel on business?

The Big Picture

YOU AREN'T PERFECT

While we all know that perfection isn't possible, we are often so busy trying to achieve it that we lose sight of the reason we thought it was so important in the first place.

In More Depth

Forget perfection. Before you get frazzled over something, ask yourself whether in 5 years (or even 5 months)—it will really matter.

Chances are, it won't.

Trying to be perfect can lead to an endless dance that ends in disillusionment and despair. Part of the problem, of course, is that we're constantly presented with examples of what "perfection" means in magazines, newspapers, and books. Many of us in the baby-boom generation were nurtured on examples of TV families that have come to stand for this perfection. In Ozzie and Harriet's world, the company was never downsized, the kids didn't get detention, and the toilet never overflowed. We know those halcyon lives aren't real, but somehow this idea of perfection remains etched in our collective social memory. Despite considerable evidence to the contrary, deep down inside many of us believe we should really be able to spend our Saturdays vacuuming the living room in pearls.

Of course, in the real world it's just not possible to juggle home, job, and kids without sometimes losing your cool. Maybe you can't do all three perfectly. It's likely you won't be perfect in *any* area. Deadlines get missed, the woodwork doesn't get washed, and you lose your temper with the kids.

That doesn't mean you're a bad parent; it simply means you're a human one. Instead of worrying over your shortcomings, accept that you aren't perfect. Shrug off the unimportant duties that are dragging you down, and try to make time for yourself, your children, your friends, and the other significant people in your lives.

Remember that what isn't nurtured soon withers away.

Mom's Point of View

Sarah, a textbook author and the mother of two sons, has long ago given up trying to be perfect. It's not that she doesn't care—she does. But she has finally realized that she will make mistakes no matter how desperately she doesn't want to. So she simply tries her best. "I'm very aware that my sons are studying me," she says. "Whatever they believe about a woman's role or a woman's capabilities, they'll first learn from me."

Sound daunting? Sarah has gotten used to this responsibility, and sees it as an opportunity to help her sons develop realistic attitudes toward women, work, and relationships. "I don't try to do everything," she says. "I admit to my limitations, but I do try to show them that if you put your mind to something, you can succeed on account of who you are, what you believe, and how hard you work."

Dad's Point of View

Harry is the father of two young boys. He has spent a lifetime trying to recover from a childhood with a father who considered himself perfect, and who expected perfection from everybody else.

"When you live with such unreasonable expectations, you come to believe that you are a failure," he says today. "It is a cruel way to bring up children." As a result, Harry loses no opportunity to let his boys know that he expects them to make mistakes. But he still finds himself coming down hard on them when they err. They can be especially demanding when he's feeling stress from work.

"The other day I spoke sharply to my younger boy for doing something I thought was wrong." His son did not argue with him, but accepted his father's anger silently, tears running down his cheeks. "It turned out I had misunderstood the whole situation, and in fact I was the one who was in the wrong." Appalled, Harry went to his son and apologized for mistakenly punishing him.

"I told him that parents make mistakes too, and that the next time I would listen more closely to his explanation. I told him that I had learned from my mistake, and I would try hard not to do it again." Harry asked his son to forgive him. "His smile almost broke my heart," Harry said.

For Reflection

When was the last time you felt that you fell short of your own expectations?

Five years from now, do you think you (or anyone else) will remember this failure?

Have you ever turned down an opportunity to be with your kids, your partner, or your friends in order to do something around the house? What would have happened if you had chosen differently?

SHARE THE JOY

It is possible to find the energy for joy in your life and to share that with your children. They need to see that you're not always hurried, harassed, and worried.

In More Depth

It takes a lot of energy to get through the day, cope with your job, come home, and focus on chores and child care. But your family will feel as if all the sacrifice is worthwhile if it's possible to avoid feeling constantly hurried and harassed.

It may seem impossible at first, but you need to try to slow down and look around. Do you enjoy your job? If so, share those feelings with your kids. Talk about the rewards of your work, what good things happened there during the day, what you enjoy most. Take them to the workplace and let them meet your coworkers, let them see what you do every day so they can understand this other role you play.

The sacrifices you make today will be rewarded when you realize your children have grown into balanced, healthy individuals who can identify with both your working and your parenting selves.

Mom's Point of View

Anne was a self-employed mom who never seemed to have enough time. What with running her 6-year-old daughter to school, activities, and parties, coping with chores, shopping, and cooking—plus her "other" job—something always seemed to be left undone. What was worse, so many times she realized that her daughter was simply left to amuse herself while Anne raced around the house trying to get things done. Even though Anne was pleased that her daughter could entertain herself with books, computer games, videos, toys, dolls, and projects, she also noticed a wistful look in her daughter's eyes now and then.

One day, after abruptly telling her daughter to find something to do so she could work, Anne heard the tiny sigh as her daughter walked away. That one sigh struck deep at her heart, and guiltily Anne remembered so many other days when she would turn away from her daughter to "get things done."

"I realized that in a just a few years, I'd have all the time in the world," Anne says. "She'd be gone, and what would it have mattered that the kitchen floor was scrubbed, or that the flowers were weeded, or even that this deadline was made on time?" All too soon, her daughter would be grown and gone, and it would be too late then for hugs and play.

"I got up from the computer, walked over to where she was sitting on the sofa, and asked her if she'd like to play. The astonished look in her eyes broke my heart." The joy with which her daughter responded to this simple gesture showed Anne that all too often, she had chosen mindless duty over the opportunity to connect.

Dad's Point of View

Troy is a heating systems repairman with a son and daughter, ages 6 and 8. His job was often physically exhausting, and when he got home at night he didn't have much time to see his two children before they went to bed. On the weekends, he liked to watch sports on TV, and resisted spending much time playing with the kids. Then he overheard his son talking with a playmate and the interaction astounded him. "My son commented very matter of factly that his daddy never played with him," Troy says. "I couldn't believe it, but I realized it was true."

Troy was particularly upset because his memories of his own childhood were marked by sadness: His own father was emotionally absent and rarely involved with Troy or his brothers. Shaken to the core, Troy realized he'd fallen into the same parenting methods by which he'd been raised.

"I'm not proud of the fact that it was easier to watch a ballgame than to sit down and play with my kids," Troy says. "I realized that I was acting just like my dad. And I had big problems with my dad when I was a teenager. I didn't want that to happen to my kids."

The very next weekend, Troy surprised his son and daughter with tickets to a softball game. He made other plans to take them to the zoo and to an auction, and the whole family planned a camping trip to the state park near their home. The family environment seems to have been revitalized by these trips. Troy had, indeed, learned to share the joy.

For Reflection

Do you find yourself pushing your kids away in favor of work, chores, and other duties?

If someone asked your children how often you play together as a family, what would they say?

Make a list of activities that you and your kids have done in the past month. Were there more than 4? Now make a list of 10 activities that you and your kids could enjoy over the next month.

CONCENTRATE ON PRIORITIES

No one can handle the multiple responsibilities of career, family, and relationship without knowing that since perfection isn't possible, some tasks must be jettisoned in order to make time for things that are truly important.

In More Depth

The "ideal" is tantalizingly seductive: We visualize the perfect mom, who comes home from a busy day in her law office in time to run the kids to scouts and hockey practice, bake cookies, and sew a party dress. Perfect dad gets home from his demanding job in time to change the baby's diapers, whip up a baked Alaska, vacuum the living room after dinner, and then settle down with a special glass of wine to toast his wife after the kids are in bed.

In reality, none of us has the time to achieve perfection in all these roles. If we concentrate on the job, chances are we have less time for the kids and no time for household responsibilities or our spouse. If we focus on the kids, our jobs may slide and the house may go to pot.

Mom's Point of View

Sue was the vice president of marketing for a training and development consulting firm that specialized in offering leadership seminars. An expert in the field, she anticipated that she could combine motherhood with her career with no problems. "I was used to achieving on many levels," she says, "and I was absolutely sure I could handle the stress of business and a child without a second thought."

Her own memories of growing up in the 1950s with a stay-at-home mom meant that Sue held a set of strong expectations about what being a good mother was. These ideals came into direct conflict when she was required to be at the office for 12- to 18-hour days in the busy season.

How would she have time to be at home with milk and cookies when her daughter came back from school? How could she volunteer at school affairs during the day, chauffeur her daughter, and whip up elegant four-course meals for her husband Steve at night?

Of course, she couldn't. It took several years for her to finally come to terms with her own expectations of what being a career woman and a mom really meant.

"I really wanted to be a stay-at-home mother like my mom," she says, "and I really wanted to achieve in my career. But each is a full-time job—you just can't be perfect in both."

What Sue finally did was to sit down with her boss and come up with a way to be able to work from home 4 days a week, communicating with the office by computer and fax. "I wasn't able to get those early images of what a good mom was out of my head," she says. "And I realized that being a good mom, to *me,* meant being available at home. This way, I can still work but I also have the time to spend with my daughter. That's my priority for today. When she goes off to college in 10 years, I'll have all the time in the world to spend on my job. My boss understands that too."

Dad's Point of View

John is a chef who thinks of himself as a perfectionist in everything he does. Still, when he became a parent he realized that there was no way that he and his wife, a legal secretary, could maintain perfection on the job, at home, and with each other.

"I take my parenting a step higher than my job," he says. "Before I was a parent or a husband, my job was the most important thing in my life. I strived to be the best in what I was doing, although I never felt I *was* the best." But these days, he doesn't allow himself to put as much pressure on himself in trying to meet his own standards.

"My parenting is the most important job I have to do, and if I have to spend a little more time or effort on something, I would definitely give the stronger effort to that." John says he doesn't feel as devoted as he once was to his job, although he's still competent. "I don't give the 110 percent effort anymore. Most of my effort goes toward my family."

In the past, failure in the kitchen would have been cause for anguish. Today, John realizes that "it's just a job. There are things that are more important. I appreciate how fortunate I am. I make the best of my family and I make bloody sure I make a good job of it."

For Reflection

List your top three priorities in life. Now look at your schedule—are you spending the most time with the things that matter most?

Do you find yourself scrambling every night to get things done, falling into bed late only to get up tired and anxious because all your responsibilities haven't been met?

How many times in the past month has mounting stress (at home, at work, or with your spouse) built up to the point where you felt like exploding?

YOU CAN DO THIS

You can do what you believe you can do. No more and no less.

In More Depth

If you spend your days worrying or criticizing yourself, you will eat away at your self-confidence to the point where you may sabotage your own performance.

The more stress you encounter and the more responsibilities you pile on yourself, the more likely it will seem that your problems have no solution. Hopelessness, quickly followed by helplessness, isn't far behind.

The trouble with this situation is that it can turn into a nasty rut, so that we dig ourselves deeper and deeper in a pit of frustration. It's at these times that there's a strong temptation to just give up.

To an amazing degree, our ability to handle rough times is related to how well we think we can do in these situations. A positive mindset may sound simplistic, but in fact the way we think about our problems can have a real effect on how well we are able to cope with them.

Mom's Point of View

No matter how bad things get, Joanne tells herself: "You can do this." That saying, she explains "is my mantra. No matter what happens or what goes wrong, I tell myself that 'I can do this' and somehow I always manage to muddle through. Things don't always work out according to plan, but they always work out. Life isn't one big fairy tale, and you shouldn't expect to live happily ever after. But that doesn't mean you have to give up and become a hermit.

"I live each day as best I can, and I raise my kids to the best of my ability. There will be weeks when all is smooth sailing and then there will be weeks where no matter what you do, everything turns out wrong.

"It's called life."

Dad's Point of View

Charles spends a lot of time caring for his daughter and works part time while his wife works full time. He admits to battling his internal ideas of male expectations and his role in this untraditional situation in which he finds himself. He is far more involved in his child's care than his father had been, but at times he's unsure of himself.

"Sometimes I lose patience with my 4 year old for no reason. I feel like I'm going to explode," he says. "I think other guys I know have the same feelings, but they don't like to admit it. It's a part of the guy package to feel like 'I can do this.'" Charles worries that these feelings are somehow unusual, that he's failing as a dad, but other men won't talk about those feelings. He believes that women would more readily understand, but adds, "I find it difficult to break into the social support circles of moms, partly from my own inner restrictions and partly from the cold shoulders I get when I try to break into chatty conversations."

Charles perseveres because he believes that his connections to his kids are an investment in the future. "Having my 4-year-old daughter come to me in the middle of the night instead of her mom really tells me something," he says. It's not a competition, but her actions show him that he's accessible to his kids in ways that many other fathers refuse to be. "So I guess, after all, I *can* do it!"

For Reflection

A positive mental attitude is really just a habit that we get into. Negative thoughts can be a tough habit to break—but recognizing the problem is the most important part.

How do you handle your thoughts when you are feeling negative? Try writing down a simple affirmation such as "I can do it" or "What's the worst that can happen?" and repeating it several times a day.

The way we approach frustration and stress can be learned. Are you teaching your kids positive ways to handle frustration and challenges?

DON'T WAIT FOR A KODAK MOMENT

Seize the moments you have with your children and make them special. When you're on the job, work hard, but when you're at home with your kids, be fully present with them.

In More Depth

You can't legislate special moments. Noted pediatrician T. Berry Brazelton recalls that he used to herd his kids into a room when he got home from work and try to *force* family togetherness. It never worked. An artificial "family time" feels just like that—artificial.

Almost all of us working parents feel guilty some of the time, aware that we spend a large part of our day away from family. The urge to try to schedule quality time can be strong. We desperately want to relate to our kids and it often feels as if there just isn't much time to do it.

But it's not a good idea to set up a specific moment with your kids. You just can't legislate the best time to get together and communicate. Instead, try to be fully present and paying attention with your kids during the everyday moments of your life, when you're riding in the car, doing the dishes, weeding the garden. You'll find that it's those times when it seems easiest and most natural to relate to your kids.

Mom's Point of View

"I'd heard so much about quality time," says Jean, a corporate attorney and mother of three children ages 8, 10, and 12. "It is frustrating and sad to me that there isn't more time, and that I'm not energetic enough to do more with the kids when there is time." As an attorney, Jean spent her whole work life subdividing her day into 15-minute time segments. When she got home after a long day at the office, she tended to see her children as another obligation that needed to be scheduled.

"I love my kids, and I was so concerned that we didn't have enough of that meaningful time together that I tried to force them to sit down and relate," she says. "They resented it. I guess it felt forced to them, and frankly they just weren't too interested. They were always busy with their own projects."

After one particularly rough day, she came home and just sat down and put her feet up. To her surprise, one by one her children came in and sat down, chatting briefly. Without organizing anything, she'd learned about their day, their thoughts and feelings. "I learned that the best way to communicate is not to wait for a special set-aside time. I make an effort to reach out to my kids on a daily basis as we go about our everyday chores. I don't try to do two jobs at once: If one wants to talk, I stop dusting or vacuuming and just listen. For me, that's the best kind of quality time there is."

Dad's Point of View

Dan is a cement contractor with one child, age 7, and he's always shared child-care responsibilities with his wife. "I'm amazed at some of the men I work with who just don't seem that interested in their kids' lives," Dan says. "They go off on weekend trips or out to play golf and shove the kids off on someone else."

Dan takes particular delight in having special "dad-daughter" activities. "I don't think you have to spend a lot of money or do extravagant things, like going to Disney World," he says. "I find one of the best things my daughter and I do together is to go get our hair cut at the same shop. Afterward I'll take her to the bookstore, and we might stop for a burger. When it's just us, she really opens up to me. I love it—just us two."

For Reflection

Sometimes parents think the amount of time they live with a child in the same house counts as quality time. Do you find yourself only half listening to your child as you run the vacuum, work on the car, or get dinner on the table?

Real communication takes attention and effort. Do you put the same attention into listening to your children that you do in communicating with your boss? With a valued customer? With a colleague or friend?

When you go home tonight, waiting for your child to come to you to initiate conversation, look at your list of activities for the evening; eliminate a few and try an impromptu chat instead. What do you think will happen?

IT'S NOT ALWAYS FAIR

Your efforts at combining child care, work, and home tasks may seem Herculean to you, but odds are your efforts won't always be universally praised. Accept that as a given, and move on.

In More Depth

We like to think that when we make sacrifices or work extra hard at breaking through society's boundaries, we'll be met with applause and congratulations. All too often, what we find is that none of this happens. Our only error is that we naively expect life to be fair.

Life is *not* fair. It can be rough, it can be unequal, and it can be unbearingly frustrating at times. Sometimes, all we can do is grit our teeth and remind ourselves that nobody promised us life would always turn out the way we expected.

Many of us run into this type of inequity when we feel we're carrying more of the family burden than our partners. It happens to people like Sherry, a receptionist for a busy pediatrician. When she's sick and stays home from work, she keeps their son Pete with her. "But when my husband is home sick," she says, "Pete goes to day care."

Mom's Point of View

One of the things that working women know intimately is that It's Not Fair. It's something that Nettie learned soon after her son was born. It was a sobering experience for her to try to learn how to cope with the baby and juggle her career at the same time. "You're competing with men who don't feel torn between home and work," she says. "And a working mom with a partner can feel like she's torn in several different ways at once."

A woman has even more problems if her spouse is a traditional husband who expects her to wait on him and take care of the house and kids. Nettie's solution? "Some days, all you can do is realize that life isn't always going to be fair. You can't always reason your problems away, ignore them, or wish them away. Some days, you just have to deal with it."

Dad's Point of View

Clarence is a self-employed dad who also takes care of a 26-month-old daughter while his wife is away at her job. Clarence had thought that he would be widely respected by women in the neighborhood, but he was stunned by the reality he faced. Women would ignore him at the park or zoo, and made it clear they had no interest in including him in their parenting discussions. His male friends assumed that because he was working at home, he was free to go fishing or travel to boat shows despite his child-care duties.

"Whenever I stood in line at the grocery store or the bank, the cashier will say 'Oh, are we babysitting today?' in a condescending voice.

"All this time I thought I'd get lots of praise for my willingness to do a woman's job,'" Clarence says ruefully. "Instead, I find little social acceptance. It may not be fair, but I let it slide off my back. The pleasure I get out of being with my daughter more than makes up for it."

For Reflection

How many times in the past month did you struggle with unfairness?

When life seems unfair, how do you react? Do you rant and rail, or glumly acquiesce? Have you come up with a coping mechanism for dealing with inequity?

What lessons do your children learn from your example in coping with unfairness?

COPE WITH TRAVEL

Coming up with contingency plans to cope with your partner's on-the-job travel will help you shoulder the burdens of responsibility.

In More Depth

When one partner's job requires extensive travel, the spouse at home often feels overburdened with responsibility and resentful at having to be both mother and father to the children.

If you and your partner face this type of uneven schedule, you need to be able to come up with a structured plan for dealing with the times when you're coping as a single parent.

Mom's Point of View

Sylvia is a law school student and the mother of a 3-year-old boy whose husband is often gone one week every month, plus additional weeks away throughout the year. Law school classes were extraordinarily stressful, and caring for her active son was exhausting, even with the babysitting help she used during the week. On the weeks when her husband was gone, she found the unrelenting necessity of parenting their son to be overwhelming.

"I got a real appreciation for how hard a job it is to be a single parent," she says, "but with the added resentment of knowing that I was married and still had to cope with these problems!" Over time, however, Sylvia came to realize that it wasn't any easier for her husband, who missed his family when he was away and felt like an outsider when he came home.

"I tried to establish a schedule, so I wouldn't feel at loose ends," she said. Knowing that everything had an appropriate time made her feel at least marginally in control. She would invite company for dinner as often as possible. "With just me and the baby, it helped to have adult conversation during dinner, even if it was to discuss the evening news, which is something my husband and I always do." Sylvia also made meals as easy as she could, preparing some ahead and freezing them for when her husband returned from work. This way, she could be sure that when her husband was home she was spending time with him and their son instead of with a cookbook and a hot stove.

Dad's Point of View

Ed was a realtor with a busy real estate firm who had the flexibility in his schedule that allowed him to stay at home and take care of his baby when his wife, a freelance researcher, had to travel on business.

An involved father, he assumed that he could fill in on short notice without any advance planning when his wife had to leave on business. He discovered it wasn't always that easy. The first time he ran into problems, his wife was gone for an entire day on business out of state, and he was left with their 3-month-old daughter. Although his wife was breast feeding, they assumed their daughter would drink formula from a bottle. The baby refused. "She screamed for 8 solid hours," Ed recalled. "She wouldn't eat anything, and I was frantic. I didn't know it was possible for a child to cry that hard for that long."

Now when his wife goes away on a trip, Ed is prepared. He writes out a schedule to make sure he knows what his daughter's normal activities are, whom she plays with, where her favorite videos are. Nothing is left to chance.

"If people could see my lists, they might think I was obsessive. But they were never left unprepared with a screaming baby!" His lists and organization give Ed a sense of control, and ensure continuity in their child's schedule.

For Reflection

If you had to go on an emergency trip for work tomorrow, would your spouse know exactly what was going on with your children?

Think of systems you could put in place to ensure continuity of child care in case either of you have to travel unexpectedly: a central calendar with appointments and dates clearly marked, important phone numbers, child's schedule, names of playmates' parents, and so on.

If your job requires frequent travel, is it worth the sacrifice? If not, what could you do to change the situation?

The Day to Day

LEARN TO DELEGATE

If you let someone else do the chores you don't have time for, you'll have more time for the things that matter most.

In More Depth

There's no such thing as supermom or superdad, and there's no way you can combine job, career, home, and child care without letting something slide. The problem that most working moms and dads face is that often, "letting something slide" feels like failure.

"My mother-in-law is a clean fanatic," says Jean, "and she always manages to pick the time to drop in when the place is looking its worst. She never says much, but I can see her looking around and noticing the socks on the floor and the dishes in the sink. I think she *enjoys* it." What Jean doesn't recognize is that in her mother-in-law's day people weren't trying to combine so many different roles at the same time.

As any good administrator will tell you, the key to good management is to delegate responsibility to those who can handle it, freeing yourself up for the most important tasks that can't be done by anyone but you.

If your kids are old enough, give them responsibility for jobs around the house—taking out the garbage, doing their laundry, picking up and even preparing some of the meals. Even the youngest toddlers can carry some items to the dinner table or pour dog food in a bowl.

What you can't delegate to family members can be handled by paid workers—hire a lawn boy or a housecleaning service, for example. If you don't feel you can afford weekly cleaning help, how about someone twice a year to help with the big jobs? Try hiring folks to do errands, take the pets to the vet, even bake dinners or lunches for the family.

Mom's Point of View

Marilyn considers herself the queen of delegation. "I believe if it's not important to the family that you do a job yourself and you can afford it, you should hire someone else to do it so you can concentrate on what's best for your family."

The busy mother of three kids ages 8, 5, and 2, Marilyn is a realtor and consultant who regularly hires others to do tasks around the house. A housecleaner comes by once a week to clean, a pet sitter takes the animals to the vets, and a lawn and pool service maintains the family's grounds.

One of her biggest problems was in remembering important birthdates and buying and mailing gifts. Now even that hassle is handled by someone else—via computer. "I subscribe to a gift-reminding service," she says. "Ten days before an important birthday, my computer reminds me of the date when I log on. I can order gifts and even cards right on-line, and have them mailed directly to the recipient."

She admits it may sound callous to do her shopping this way, but what it all means is that she has more time for her children and her husband. "And to me, that's the bottom line. Nothing is more important than having time for my family."

Dad's Point of View

Of course, delegating is not always an easy solution. To some people—especially hands-on perfectionists like Tom, a busy young architect—giving responsibility to someone else feels like a loss of control.

"I like to make sure everything is done the way I like it," he says, "and that usually means doing it myself. I'm happier that way, because then I know it will be right."

A few summers ago, when some local boys came around looking for lawn-mowing jobs, Tom turned them down. "I like doing it myself," he told his exasperated wife, who was starting to complain because it took Tom all weekend to mow their 4 acres of lawn—and that didn't count the trimming. "I didn't think they would do a good job," he said. "I like the lawn to be mowed diagonally, and in a different direction each week." He had the same response when his wife suggested hiring help to steam-clean the carpets, paint the living room, fix the washer, and re-cover the living room sofa.

But as their son and daughter grew older, new demands were placed on the family's weekend. Eventually, there just wasn't time to do all the chores around the house and still be with the family he loved. As his wife and kids began to spend more time doing things without him, Tom decided to reconsider his stance.

"I finally realized that it's okay not to have everything perfect, or everything the way I want. What good is it to have the most perfect lawn in the neighborhood if my kids don't know me anymore?"

For Reflection

How much time would you save if you hired people to help with some of your chores around the house?

What would happen if you asked family members to do more of the work around the house?

How many times must you interrupt your work time to deal with a problem at home?

SPEND FREE TIME WISELY

Remember to nurture not just your children, but your own relationship with your partner.

In More Depth

Often working parents feel so guilty about spending time away from their children that when they do get some free time, they feel duty-bound to spend every moment with their kids. Healthy marriages need nurturing too, and that requires some time with just the two of you.

The whole point of using your free time wisely is to have more of it to spend with your children, your partner, and yourself. Of course, some working parents insist they don't have *any* free time to give to anyone. If this is your situation, look more closely at your schedule. Could you get up a half-hour earlier in the morning? Go to bed a bit later in the evening? Cut back on volunteer time?

Mom's Point of View

Abbie and her husband Bill are high school teachers and coaches with two teenaged girls. Their lives were full of school, work, ballet lessons, riding lessons, and chores.

"I was convinced that our lives were so packed with activities that we didn't have one spare moment for spontaneous fun," she says. When Abbie got home from school, she put in an hour or so of grading papers and chauffeuring her daughters. She would try to vacuum or throw in a load of wash. After dinner there was more homework to read, lessons to plan, and chores to finish. All weekend was spent doing yard work, working in the garden, running the girls to appointments, and doing more errands and chores.

As their lives got more frenetic, Abbie realized that the family was spending a great deal of time simply spinning wheels. She decided a new approach was needed. First, when she and her husband got home from school they set a timer for 30 minutes. During that time, they would pick a room and clean it; when the timer rang, they would stop cleaning and begin preparing dinner. "Something about the set time for cleaning somehow made it more of a manageable job," she says. "You didn't tend to put it off because it was overwhelming." Since they did this every night, before long the house was far more tidy and required less attention each day. Their weekends were now freed from cleaning chores.

Next, she required her girls to do their own laundry and iron their own clothes, and be responsible for cleaning their own rooms.

Since free time has a way of disappearing, Abbie started scheduling the family's new-found leisure time on her calendar. Weekend camping trips, exercise, and dinner out were all written down to make sure nothing else interfered. "It seemed a little silly to write down something like 'walk with Bill after dinner'—but planning for this free time was the only way we'd use it wisely." She also used the calendar to block out an hour or two for a leisurely bath or an afternoon of reading. "Somehow, if it was on the calendar, I didn't feel so *guilty* spending time on myself."

Dad's Point of View

Allan is a busy plumbing contractor who feels as if he has to be doing something all the time. He works hard during the week, and when he gets home at night and on weekends he can't seem to relax. "There are always things to be done around the house," says Allan, who built his own home and spends many hours working on projects that need to be done around the house. He spent all his spare time on making further improvements—things at which he felt he could excel.

While he loves his family, Allan realized he was always so busy doing chores that there was never any time left over for family on the weekends. "I realized that the only time I really stop doing these *projects* is when we're away," Allan said. When he saw how depressed his preoccupation with chores was making his wife, the two discussed what could be done.

"We realized that what we needed were a few brief vacations scattered throughout the year," he says. They scheduled one week at the beach in early summer and a long weekend at the beach in early fall. In between they break out more long weekends for getaways at favorite haunts. On New Year's Day, the two sit down and plan more long weekends at other times of the year so that there is never too long a time between breaks.

"Having something to look forward to has made all the difference," Allan says. "When you're having a bad patch, it really helps to know that you'll be able to get away in a couple of weeks."

For Reflection

Keep a detailed log of how you spend every moment during one weekend. Account for everything—*you'll learn a great deal about how you use your time and how time gets wasted.*

Go through the calendar and find a few odd long weekends to plan some getaway breaks. Write them down and treat them as important dates, every bit as vital as work conferences or job interviews.

Figure out how much free time you have each week, and set aside on your calendar an hour or two for a personal break, a couple break, and a kid break.

LEARN TO LISTEN

We all need to listen more often to our kids, but this is especially important for those youngsters who will be staying home alone while mom and dad are at work.

In More Depth

It sounds easy, but actually very few people really listen with intensity when someone else is talking. Doubt it? Have you every praised someone for "making you feel like you're the only person in the room" when you were talking to that person? Most likely, it's because the person was listening to you with intensity, really hearing what you were saying.

Most of the time—and often with our kids—we arrive home preoccupied with work stress. How often do you stop really listening, filling in the information or thinking about what you're going to say while others are still talking? How many of us get busy with chores around the house while our child is talking to us, so that we find ourselves answering "uh-huh" with a distracted tone?

It doesn't take long for this type of distracted attention to frustrate and eventually distance our kids. It's not always easy to listen closely to an elementary school child prattle on endlessly—but if you turn away now, it's a sure bet that the lines of communication will come down permanently by the time your child is a teenager. It's especially important to listen closely if your child is spending time alone after school, to make sure you can pick up on problems if they occur.

Mom's Point of View

Sue thinks of herself as a good, concerned mother. But once she leaves work and gets home where her 11-year-old is waiting for her, she must get dinner, pick up, clean the house, and start the laundry—and she's often still distracted by work problems. It's usually this time that her daughter chooses to want to talk.

"The other day my daughter was showing me some artwork she had done, and I barely glanced at it," Sue says. "I was busy trying to figure out whether I should defrost the hamburger or just have spaghetti without meatballs. It was late, and I could see the floor needed to be scrubbed." When Sue's daughter showed her the art, Sue simply said "Uh-huh" in a distracted tone.

"I'm really proud of this," her daughter said angrily, "and you barely looked at it!" Her daughter's honesty and injured tone immediately stopped Sue in her tracks. "Here I was fussing over hamburger and a menu, and I was completely missing something that obviously meant something to my daughter." It hadn't been the best time to show off artwork, Sue admits, but "with kids, you need to grab those moments. In another year or two, I realized that she might not even bother to show me stuff from school if I appear to be too distracted to care."

It was a moment that Sue felt deeply. "The fact that she gets home alone means she's already alone for too long a time. I don't need to add to that loss by being emotionally absent while I'm right in the room."

Dad's Point of View

"My Dad never had time for me," says Bob, an addictions counselor. "I can't think of one time when he actually sat down and listened to my problems." It was something that he had vowed would never happen in *his* family; indeed, his entire career is focused on the ability to listen. So he was astonished when his wife began to complain that he wasn't listening to her or the kids.

"As soon as I'd walk in the door, I'd get hit with the problems my wife had been storing up all day," Bob explained. Since she got home an hour before he did, she'd already had her hands full with their two children, ages 8 and 10. When Bob got home, she tended to vent her pent-up frustration.

"It's not easy being an addictions counselor, and a lot of my colleagues burn out," he said. "Sometimes it gets so exhausting listening to people's problems all day long. Sometimes when I get home, I feel like if I hear one more problem, I'll explode."

Ashamed of these feelings, Bob kept silent rather than tell his wife he didn't want to listen to her. It was so important to him not to follow in his father's footsteps that he couldn't envision himself turning his back on his wife. But he realized one day this was exactly what he was doing.

"Our older girl was telling me about something that had happened that day, and I had totally turned her out. I was staring past her with my mind a blank, when I caught her looking at me. She said 'Dad! You haven't heard a word I said!' I felt I was turning into my father, all over again."

As a counselor, Bob had enough self-awareness to understand his problem was not that he didn't *want* to listen, but that sometimes he just *couldn't*—his circuits were simply overloaded. He needed some time after work to decompress, leave his office issues behind, and move into his "husband and father mode." After discussing the problem with Mary, they decided he should take a half hour after work to shower, get a soda, and sit down to look through the paper before confronting problems. Thus refreshed, he would be better able to invest emotionally in whatever problems or situations needed to be discussed.

"It's hard to believe that such a small adjustment could make such a big difference," Bob says, "but Mary noticed an improvement right away. And now my kids know that once I've eased off the tensions of the day, I'm always ready to listen."

For Reflection

How often in the last week did you listen to your children automatically, thinking about what you were going to say before they'd finished talking?

Can you think of ways that you could improve your listening skills?

Listen to your kids tonight. Are they telling you the truth, or only what they think you want to hear?

MAKE TIME FOR FUN

Beware of the tyranny of the "shoulds" in your life. Responsibility is one thing, but realize that while duties don't disappear, opportunities will.

In More Depth

Almost all of us has the ability to enjoy life a little bit more, carve out some time for ourselves, and most important—learn how to make time for fun. Soon enough we'll all have plenty of time for manicures and golf, and we'll be looking back on the days of sweeping up Cheerios off the floor with nostalgia. Childhood is really just a collection of these evanescent moments that are too soon past.

Mom's Point of View

Cecelia was an administrative secretary who never had time for fun in her life. Her daily schedule looked like a timetable for a marine recruit: She got up at 5:30 A.M., showered, dressed, got her daughter up and dressed, left home at 7 A.M., dropped her daughter off at day care, worked until 5:30 P.M., picked up her daughter on the way home, made dinner, read a bedtime story, gave her daughter a bath, tucked her in bed, retucked her in, and then fell into bed, exhausted, at 9:30 P.M. She had no time for fun, for her husband, for TV, books, movies—nothing except her daily routine.

Something had to give before her sanity did. "I woke up one day and couldn't get out of bed," she says. "I felt as if one more day on the treadmill and I would just go mad."

Her solution was to take a long, hard look at her schedule and eliminate some of the built-in stress, in part by forgetting some of the "shoulds" and in part by enlisting the help of her husband. First, she decided to shower the night before so she could save considerable time in the rushed mornings. Since she was responsible for driving her daughter to and from day care, her husband took over the job of getting her ready to go—dressing and breakfast chores. Cecelia really didn't want to give up bedtime stories or tuck-ins, but the chore of cooking dinner every night was unpleasant. Her solution?

"On Wednesdays it's Pizza Night," she says. "I pick up a pizza on the way home—no cooking, no washing dishes. On Friday, it's a restaurant, just the three of us." They usually choose inexpensive family places—sometimes it's fast food—with an emphasis on spending fun time together. On Mondays and one weekend night, Cecelia's husband cooks. Since she now stays in bed until 6:15 A.M., she can stay up later at night and enjoy a book or a rented video. And she and her husband set one weekend day aside just to play with their daughter, visit the zoo, or go for a walk in the park.

"I can deal with a stressful schedule much better now that I have some help, and that I know on the weekend we'll be able to have some fun time for us."

Dad's Point of View

John is a busy ophthalmologist who grew up in a single-parent home with little money and less time for pleasure. The oldest of five brothers and sisters, he learned early on the value of hard work and discipline—to the point where he now finds it difficult to simply kick back and have fun.

"Most of the time," he says, "my wife was the one who would plan the vacations and the excursions. I'd go along, but they were never my idea. I was always working, and I felt like I should spend my weekends working around the house. Taking time to do fun things felt like a lack of responsibility; I was always anxious to get back to work."

Then one day he overheard his young daughter ask her mother: "How come Daddy never laughs?"

John realized that he spent so much time doing things for his family there was little time to simply enjoy them. He decided to set Sunday aside as "family day," when he would do no work around the house. Instead, the three went to zoos, parks, and other attractions—and he and his wife took turns planning the trips. He found that when he was responsible for planning a family day, he got a much bigger kick out of participating. "All that time I thought I was working hard for my family," he said, "but I didn't have a clue what I was missing."

For Reflection

When was the last time you kicked over the traces and did something just for fun?

Make a list of three things you and your family could do this weekend that don't involve chores, responsibility, or unpleasantness—ideally, things you haven't recently done.

Get into the habit of asking yourself "Why not?" when your child wants to do something a little bit out of the ordinary. Once a week or once a month, try to think up an activity that your family has never done before, and do it.

FIND QUALITY TIME

Quality time doesn't require hours of dedication—a small space here and there of dedicated one-on-one attention does a lot for your child.

In More Depth

One of the most common frustrations that working parents report is the lack of time and attendant guilt for focusing so little of it on their children. When you get home from work, there's the house to clean, the bills to pay, and dinner to get on the table, and then comes the rush of homework, baths, and bedtime rituals. Where is the time to simply sit and enjoy the kids?

Parents who already feel torn with guilt for placing their children in day care are haunted by the time they must spend on other responsibilities once they arrive home. "Sometimes it seems as if there are 100 priorities and no time to take care of them," one dad complained.

It may help to know that "quality time" doesn't mean you have to dedicate an entire afternoon toward some special event, although your child would certainly enjoy the treat. Try to find moments of calm when you can concentrate on your child, and always be on the lookout for ways to include the youngster in everyday activities.

Mom's Point of View

Betsy is a working mom who doesn't get home from the city until 6:30 P.M., when she picks up her 2-year-old daughter from the babysitter down the street. Betsy's husband doesn't get home until 11:00 P.M., so the full brunt of the home and child-care responsibilities falls on Betsy's shoulders. Since her daughter goes to bed by 8:30 P.M., it's a real challenge to get the child fed and bathed, much less spend much time in play. "It seemed as if I was in a mad rush from the moment I got in the door until I got her in bed," she says. "Then I felt bad that we didn't have enough time together."

Eventually, she realized that if she was going to have any special time with her daughter she'd have to come up with ways to include her. She has discovered that if she sits down with her daughter the minute she gets home, the child is content for a while to let mom get some chores done while dinner is cooking. As dinner progresses, she stands on a chair by the counter, playing with safe toys like plastic measuring cups and water.

Betsy also realized that she spent much of the time on weekends doing household chores and running errands. She decided to hire cleaning help twice a month in order to free herself for play on the weekends. "It seems like an extravagance to pay someone else to clean," she says, "but I realized that having time with my daughter while she's young is far more important. By not eating lunch out in restaurants, I can use that money for cleaning help. This buys me the time to get to know my daughter better. It's worth it to me!"

Dad's Point of View

Many times, a busy schedule can put a crimp in the amount of time you have to spend with your kids. Many dads in particular find that they have only a few hours a day to see their children. While this was accepted as normal in the 1950s, today many working dads object to spending so much of their time away from home.

Ross is a bank vice president whose long hours mean he gets to see his 5-year-old son for only about an hour and a half a day through the week. "My wife doesn't realize how little time that is," he says. "Because she's self-employed, she takes our son to school and back, and fits her schedule around him. My time with him is usually organized around dinner, bathing, and bed."

Because he had so little amount of time with his son to begin with, Ross realized that he would have to make the time he did have count. He couldn't do much about the weekdays, but on the weekends he focused on spending special time with his son.

"We play school, and I focus on things he's doing in kindergarten or things he needs help with. We talk, we play together—just the two of us—and I don't do anything else at the same time." When Ross is playing with his son, the lawn goes unmowed and the car doesn't get washed. "Sometimes I'm tempted to read a magazine while we play a game, but I realize that means I'm not totally focused on my son. I have so little time with him, that dividing what time we have would be cheating."

For Reflection

In the past week, how often did you sit down with your children and spend time with them, one on one?

Can you think of things you could do differently when you get home from work so that you could spend a little extra time with your kids?

How would life at your house be different if you spent an hour a day less on home chores, and an hour a day more interacting with your children and your spouse?

FOCUS ON SMALL ISSUES

The big picture often takes care of itself. If you really want to see some changes, try focusing on the small issues.

In More Depth

If you're not happy with the way you and your family are struggling to handle home and work issues, you may be trying to do too much. Having great expectations—or demanding global change from a partner—may mean you're setting yourself up for failure. When we're stressed and frustrated and lashing out in anger, we tend to make those broad indictments that sound good at the time but aren't very effective in changing things. You'll know you're approaching things in the wrong way if you're using the *never* and *always* words: "You never help around the house" or "You always nag me to death."

Instead, focus on small, tangible ways that you or your partner could work on problems. Instead of demanding that your spouse "stop living like a pig" or "help around the house"—just exactly what does that mean?—be specific. "Honey, let's split the meal chores: I'll cook and you can do the dishes."

Mom's Point of View

Peri is a full-time interior designer with three kids ages 20 months to 6 years. While she and her husband, a building contractor, share child-care duties fairly well, there have been times when things just didn't work. In the beginning of their marriage when their first child was small, Peri recalls that her husband just wasn't interested in helping out around the house. "He didn't want to give the baby a bottle while I got dressed because it 'interfered with his morning routine' of drinking coffee and looking out the window," she says.

What worked for her, she says, is that she "started small." Instead of demanding that he share all the child-care duties, she began by asking him to do one small job related to child care. "Pick your battles carefully," she advises. "I realized that my husband had no idea that his help could be very valuable to me."

Today, he gets up before Peri does, fixes breakfast for the children, gets the baby dressed, and packs lunchboxes for the kids. He also takes their son to school and picks him up so Peri doesn't have all three to drop off at different locations.

Dad's Point of View

Simon and Leah had been married for 7 years with one son, age 5. While they generally got along fairly well, little annoyances had been building up for some time. Since neither partner liked to argue, the little irritations seldom were resolved, but continued to build up.

"There seemed to be a low level of tension around the house," Simon says, "and it got to the point where we would blow up over nothing. Or what seemed like nothing." Simon realized that the problem they both had in handling anger meant they bottled up their feelings and didn't deal with the "small" stuff.

"For my anniversary present to my wife, I told her to make a list of all the annoying little things I did that she didn't like. I wouldn't argue or disagree; I'd just work on each one and try to stop doing the things she didn't like." When Simon convinced Leah that he really meant what he said, they sat down and discussed some of the petty annoyances that got under each of their skins, and both resolved to work on them.

"No matter how much you agree on the major stuff," Simon says, "it's always the little things that really start getting to you. While you may not be able to do much about those things on a job, at home you should be able to work through these problems."

For Reflection

Think back over the last few fights that you've had with your partner. Did they start over a major issue, or was it merely small insignificant irritations?

Identify five things you do that you think bothers your partner. What would happen if you tried to change your behavior in these things?

What do you need to do in order to improve the way the "little things" are managed in your home?

MAKE TIME FOR MEMORIES

We remember moments, not lifetimes. Even the busiest of working parents can give the gift of memories to their children that will last a lifetime.

In More Depth

Your report isn't done, the boss is on the rampage, the lawn mower broke, and the baby has the croup: It's a typical day for a working parent. Given the never-ending stress and crises of our lives, sometimes the job of parenting can seem overwhelming.

You must accept the fact that things will *never* be perfect—there will always be stress on the job, there will always be problems at home, there will always be a crisis at one time or another with a child. If you can't do it all, you must just do what's important. Spend time with your kids, and give them the most generous gift of all: your time. Toys get lost and broken, but memories last a lifetime.

Older parents whose kids are grown are surprised that what their children remember from childhood seemed like nothing special to the grownups at the time: making cookies each December, going fishing at Uncle Ned's, visiting Cousin Emily's farm. To an adult, these are everyday kinds of activities. To a child, they are magic transmuted into memory.

Mom's Point of View

Anastasia is a working mom and a college student with three children ages 10, 5, and 2. Because of her busy schedule, she has only about 5 hours a day to spend with her children. This quickly taught her what was worth fighting over and what wasn't.

Each week, each child spends a "special time" with mom for about a half-hour, which the three of them look forward to all week. "I turn off the TV, the computer, everything. I don't answer the door. I make the children feel important and special, and they get to decide what to do." Because this is "special time," if they want to make a mess, Anastasia lets them—reasoning that it will last for only a half hour.

She also tries to juggle the routine, driving home a different way and pointing out the new scenery. "Sometimes we go to grandma's, and visit on a weeknight instead of a weekend." Since grandmother always loves to see the grandkids, it gets Anastasia out of fixing dinner one night a week! Sometimes they spread a blanket on the floor and have a picnic in the kitchen, playing a tape of birds singing in the background. The kids cut out green construction paper "grass" and sprinkle it on the blanket. "All of this may sound a little unorthodox," she says, "but what's more important—family life to remember or whether the dishes are done? They're never really done, anyway. There will always be more tomorrow."

Dad's Point of View

Sometimes there's nothing really wrong with a family's life together—but there isn't much excitement either. It's easy to get into a rut of school and work, homework, dinner, bedtime, chores, and responsibilities. When Andy realized that this was happening to his family, he decided to do something about it.

"When I remember fun times in my childhood, it's always the unexpected, the unusual, that sticks in my mind. I wanted to give our kids some memories of things we did as a family that were out of the ordinary."

What Andy did was to begin a "Pajama Ride" for his kids. Every month or two—usually on a weekend night—after the kids would get into their pajamas and into bed, Andy and his wife would march into the kids' bedroom singing "pajama ride, pajama ride" at the tops of their voices.

Everyone would pile into the car—kids in their pajamas—and they'd be off on their adventure. Sometimes they'd drive to a local ice cream place and get cones to eat under the stars. Sometimes they'd drive out to a country hill with a good view and look at the stars. If they didn't stop for food along the way, Andy would be sure to stock up on popcorn, pretzels, or a thermos of hot cocoa to drink on the trip. "We didn't go on big trips," Andy says. "The key wasn't the exotic destination, it was the fun of thinking you had to go to bed and then finding out you were going on an adventure that made it fun."

For Reflection

Think back to your own childhood and recall what some of your happiest memories were as a family. Why were they so happy?

Is it possible to re-create some of those memories for your own kids? Make a list of 10 things you might try in the future that would help make good memories for your family.

Trips to Disney World are big fun, but memories are made up of emotions as well as experiences. Start thinking of little things you can do that will foster happy memories for your children.

JUST DO IT!

Work is hard. Parenting is hard. But part of what makes great effort worthwhile is the reward it brings when you triumph over the hardships.

In More Depth

Real babies get sick. They throw up on your best suit as you're going out the door to that important meeting. They break out in chicken pox on the day the vital brief is due on the partner's desk. And just when you think you've convinced the boss that you can indeed "do it all," in the middle of a sales presentation you get a frantic call from the day-care center telling you that your daughter has pushed a pea up her nose and seems to be having trouble breathing.

Being a two-career couple with a family is not easy. But nobody ever said that handling three full-time jobs—home, career, and family—would be anything other than near impossible.

Once you've decided to take on the commitment, sitting around whining about it is simply a waste of time. Odds are, it's time you don't have to spare. Like the sneaker commercial says—Just Do It! Twenty years from now, you'll be glad you did.

Mom's Point of View

Jean operated a small day-care business in her home for 9 years during the time her own two children were young. "There were days when the stress of doing day care and watching my own kids made me want to scream," she says. "But what choice did I have? I needed to work, and I couldn't afford day care myself."

Trying to cope with all those children at the same time was exhausting. She felt as if she never had any privacy, since parents were constantly coming in and out of her house. She also found that many parents didn't seem to respect her. One year, she wasn't able to go on vacation because one of the parents threatened to leave if she took 2 weeks off. Since Jean couldn't afford to lose the client, she acquiesced. Jean's family did not go on vacation that year.

"It was nice to be able to stay home with my children," she recalls. "But there were times that it was very, very hard. You do what you have to do to make things work."

Dad's Point of View

George is a midlevel manager who gave up a lucrative position because the long hours meant that he would have less time to spend with his family. "I think it's important to keep personal goals and ambitions in mind, but they have to have their place. Responsibility as a parent means your parenting duties must come first. If you want to be a parent, you have to be prepared to assume the role with all the pleasures and responsibilities. Tears and sunshine come with it."

He copes with the frustrations of the present lower-paying job by dividing his week into segments whenever the work isn't going well. He goes from morning to lunch, from lunch to the evening. And then he is rewarded by going home and seeing his wife and daughter.

"When you take on the task of parenthood, you take on the whole load," he says, "whatever it's going to be. And you stick with it and see it through. If you don't do that, you're not a parent."

For Reflection

When times seem hard, remember that in a few years the kids will be grown and gone, and all your current frustrations will pass away.

If you're feeling overwhelmed, stop and think how much harder things were for our great-grandparents, when laundry was boiled, clothes were all made by hand, and many children never lived past infancy.

When things get frustrating, stop and ask yourself what you would be doing if you weren't a parent, if you'd never known your son or daughter.

SAY GOOD-BYE TO GUILT

There is no reason to feel guilty for doing what you have to do in order to provide for your family.

In More Depth

Many parents don't have the luxury of living on one salary; in order to survive, both mom and dad must work. When there are small children in the home, this often means that they will spend part of the day in some type of day-care or babysitting arrangement.

This necessity causes almost unbearable guilt for many working moms and dads, who face the daily leave taking with wrenching pain. "When he cries and doesn't want me to leave, it breaks my heart," one mom said.

But studies show that good day care is not harmful to kids who come from healthy, loving homes. Indeed, many children blossom with the chance of interacting with their peers in an enriched environment. If you're faced with the necessity of work and day care, try to realize that you're doing what you believe is best for your family.

What children really need are confident parents, says pediatrician T. Berry Brazelton, M.D., not a parent at home for any specified length of time. If you're going to be at work thinking you should be at home, your child will pick up on that. If you're going to be at home wishing you were at work, your child will pick up on that too.

Mom's Point of View

Cecelia is a busy mom whose days are spent at work and whose nights are spent at school, working toward a degree. While the thought of day care made her uncomfortable at first, she's come to see that it is right for her family.

"Based on what I've seen, I think there are trade-offs," she says. "Our daughter seems happy and well adjusted." In fact, Cecelia thinks her daughter has benefitted from being attended to by trained caregivers.

"I don't believe I would have some special power to make her life better if it were just the two of us," she says. "In fact, her caregivers have much more experience than I do." She notes that it was a day-care worker who taught Cecelia's daughter things her mother never dreamed she was old enough to learn. "She learned how to blow her nose and throw away the tissue way before it dawned on me she could do it."

Dad's Point of View

David is a midlevel marketing manager who says he wishes he or his wife could stay home with their son and daughter. "It's probably harder on my wife, since she's the one that society says should stay home with them. She says she feels like stay-at-home moms look down on her." David's own mother has occasionally complained that people who have to use day care should think about that before they have kids. "It's a different world today," David tells her. "People just can't make it on only one salary."

David says he worries about the colds his kids bring home from day care, and about the fact that they have to get up so early in the morning in order to be dropped off. "But we simply don't have any choice if we don't want to live in a box on the street," he says. "And my kids seem happy. That's the bottom line to me."

For Reflection

Worry comes with the parenting territory. If you didn't send the kids to day care, would there be something else you would worry about?

Make a list of 10 skills your child has learned since attending day care. How many of them were taught by the day-care workers?

At the end of the day, does your child seem happy and content?

LISTEN TO THE SILENCE

"If we have not paused with our children in silence this day, how will we know we are truly alive? How will we know, unless we have heard one another's breath and heartbeat?"

—***Shea Darian***, Seven Times the Sun

In More Depth

We all need a break from the chaos of daily life. With the pull of work, chores, and endless errands, we are constantly at risk of loosening our family's bond. Added to these daily burdens is the nonstop electronic interference from TV, radio, stereos, videos, computers, and electronic games. Today it's possible for all our family members to be home, each isolated before a flickering screen and oblivious to everyone else.

By spending some time in quiet listening, we can knit up the unraveling threads of our life's tapestry.

Mom's Point of View

Like many parents, Mary was concerned about the amount of time her sons spent playing Nintendo and other video games. One day when the noise from the living room was particularly obnoxious, Mary suddenly recalled an afternoon she had spent several years ago at Gallaudet University in Washington, D.C.

Mary is a freelance writer who had been doing research at Gallaudet, the largest U.S. university for deaf students. "The campus is located in a fairly blighted area of downtown D.C.," Mary recalls, "but I remember that as soon as I walked onto the grounds, how peaceful everything was." She was particularly struck by the total silence. It was something she never forgot.

She realized it was something her own family needed. "When things get noisy around the house, I go in and ask the boys to turn off the games for awhile. Then we play the "Listen to the Silence" game. We sit quietly, eyes closed, and just listen. Then we try to name the sounds we hear. If we can't figure out the source, we track it down." It's a game that is especially good to play outdoors, where so many sounds are often ignored.

"We all get so busy with work and school," she says, "that it's nice just to stop and listen together."

Dad's Point of View

The noisy environment of the print shop was stressful for Ted, a press foreman. When he got home, the last thing he wanted to have to listen to was the blaring noise from TV and stereos. One of the biggest annoyances in his life came from modern technology—the video, TV, and computers that vied for his daughter's attention.

"We have so little time together as a family," he says. The family goes off early to school and work, and then there's the rush of dinner at 6:00 P.M. Bedtime comes at 7:30 P.M., and then the whole routine begins again the next day. Their schedule is tight enough, Ted realized, but what made it worse was that the little free time they did have was frittered away in electronic isolation.

"As soon as my daughter gets home from school she races to turn on a video, and she watches the same ones over and over," he says. "On the weekends, I watch ball games on TV. And every night and most weekends my wife is on the computer." In the midst of the noise blaring from TV, CDs, and stereos, Ted realized his family was slowly, inexorably, growing apart.

Instead of trying to forcibly drag everyone from various electronic pursuits, he suggested during dinner one night that they begin a daily family "quiet time." They decided to start after dinner: In winter, they would sit together, light a candle, and work on quiet pursuits such as stringing beads, weaving baskets, knitting, or using watercolors. In summer, they would go for "silent walks" around the neighborhood, picking a comfortable spot along the way to sit in silence and listen to nature. "It really rejuvenated everyone," he says.

For Reflection

How much time do you spend together as a family in quiet times? How much time are you involved in electronic pursuits?

If you lost your electric power tomorrow, would you be able to find things to do with your family?

What stories did your grandparents tell you about how they amused themselves before the advent of TV and computer?

Partner Techniques

SHARE THE LOAD

Dividing household and child-care chores equally gives you both some free time and avoids one partner feeling overloaded, abused, and unappreciated.

In More Depth

"Sharing household jobs" sounds easy. But one of the most contentious areas working parents face is the problem of who does what, and when, and how often.

In a two-career family, studies have shown that the majority of housework chores still fall to the woman, who has traditionally borne the mantle of "homemaker." It is a situation that can bitterly divide a family. And even the most modern couples who successfully divide household responsibilities BTC (before the children) may find that their jobs break down along traditional gender lines when baby arrives. Dads who used to clean the bathroom and moms who used to tote out the garbage cans suddenly find themselves looking and sounding more like Ozzie and Harriet.

But when both parents have to get up for work in the morning, both must be willing to spend some hours at night with housework and comforting, feeding, and tucking in little ones.

Mom's Point of View

Cheryl always thought of herself as a modern, liberated woman and vowed never to follow in the footsteps of her mother, who had been a traditional wife and mother. "I never dreamed I'd be in a relationship where everything isn't 50-50." Indeed, Cheryl's husband was delighted that she wanted to keep her own name after their marriage, and he shared her vision of equality within the relationship. But after their first baby was born, things seemed to change. "After working all day, I came home to do the laundry, cook the meals, clean the house, fold and put away clothes, pick up, vacuum, scrub the tub—and John changed the oil in the car twice a year. I tried not changing our bed once to see how long it would take before *he* changed the sheets, but after a month I couldn't stand it anymore."

Finally, Cheryl confronted her husband, who insisted he felt he shared equally in the chores. "He did do much more than the other guys he worked with, but that's only because they didn't do *anything*," she said. When Cheryl questioned John, she discovered that much of her work simply went unnoticed. She got home first, and spent an hour or two cleaning—which her husband never knew. When he would pack their daughter's lunch, vacuum the house once or twice a month, and occasionally do the dinner dishes, he cited that as sharing equally. It wasn't until they actually kept a log of chores each performed that he was able to see he wasn't really pulling his weight. Since then, they have assigned responsibility for particular jobs so that everything gets done equally.

Of course, sharing the chores doesn't mean you have to stick to rigid rules: "You've given the baby two fewer bottles than I did, so you owe me two." Instead, aim for flexibility and try to sense when your partner has had too much. Don't wait for your partner to feel overworked and stressed out. Does dad have a big presentation tomorrow? Then mom should take over his night feeding chore. Is mom scheduled to appear in court the next day? Then dad should get up when a child comes crying for comfort with a nightmare.

Dad's Point of View

Owner of his own business, Daniel is a successful pharmacist with a clearly defined sense of order. "I can't function in chaos," he says. "Maybe it's my job, but at work everything must be extremely precise. There isn't any room for mistakes. I guess I bring those feelings home. I just feel more comfortable with everything in its place."

Unfortunately, Daniel's innate orderliness is at odds with his wife Judy's more laissez-faire attitude. A home economist, Judy's home office is littered from floor to ceiling with books, papers, magazines, and articles to clip. The rest of the house would have looked like her office if it weren't for Dan, who regularly swept through and picked up everything in his wake.

"I think Judy just assumed that since it's my nature to be neat, I didn't mind carrying the whole load of straightening up and doing the chores," he said. "She would tell me it didn't bother her when the dishes didn't get done right away, so I'd end up doing them, and resenting it."

But as their three children got older, Daniel felt even more stress as he struggled to clean up Judy's mess and handle the lion's share of the chores after spending a stressful day at the pharmacy.

"Then one day I read an article in a woman's magazine about getting your spouse to help with the chores," he confessed, "and I realized it didn't have to be this way." Daniel sat down with Judy and explained how much he resented having to carry the load for the household.

They agreed that Daniel would stop complaining about the state of Judy's office if she would try to do more chores in the rest of the house. Judy would keep her office door closed so it wouldn't matter how messy it was. The responsibility for the rest of the house was divided more equally.

Since certain areas of the home—like a sparkling bathroom—really mattered to Daniel, he took over those duties where he could keep things exactly as he liked. Judy agreed to handle chores for the living room, dining room, and den, which seemed more manageable to her.

Now that their expectations are clearer, Daniel says things are much more pleasant around the house. He's happy because the house is neater and he's not doing all the work, and Judy is happy because Daniel's not on her back about the chores.

For Reflection

Ask your partner if he or she thinks you share chores equally. Do you both agree?

Odds are there will be a discrepancy between your assessments. Can you come up with a method of dividing chores more evenly? Possibilities include:

- *Make a "job jar" filled with necessary jobs. Each of you pull out a job to do that week.*
- *Assign jobs to both of you, and next week switch jobs.*
- *Try the "you choose, I pick" method. Have one person divide the jobs into two groups, and have the other pick the group to work on that week.*
- *Assign rooms for each of you to clean each week. Stipulate that these rooms must be cleaned before anything else can be done on the weekend.*

If all else fails, could you hire a cleaning service?

TAKE A BREAK!

Just as we all need vacations from our jobs to refresh ourselves, so we as parents need an occasional break from our child-care responsibilities.

In More Depth

No parent would disagree that raising children is the hardest job we'll ever have. Why, then, do so many of us have a problem admitting we need an occasional break from the responsibility? Who hasn't spent an afternoon with three cranky, fighting siblings without gazing out the window and wondering what the weather is like in Ibiza?

Too often, these wistful yearnings make us feel guilty. *They shouldn't!* Taking a brief break from the kids—even if it's only an hour or so away—can refresh you and help you deal more lovingly with the next crisis.

Mom's Point of View

Sandy is a department store saleswoman who spends part of her week at home with her two children, ages 2 and 4. There are days when coping with two youngsters this close in age is almost overwhelming. One day it all seemed just too much. The only word Sam, the 2-year-old, had uttered all day was "No!" and he screamed it each time at the top of his voice. No, he didn't want to get dressed, eat his cereal, share a doughnut with his sister. Meanwhile 4-year-old Sally had been whining and difficult in her own right, constantly coming to Sandy for attention and trying to push her little brother out of the picture. By 2:00 P.M. that day, when she found Sally in Sam's bedroom grappling over a Power Ranger action figure, Sandy was ready to give up and send them both to day care.

At that moment Sandy's husband Harry walked in the door. He'd arranged to work half a day that afternoon to give his wife a break, and as Sandy grabbed her purse and almost ran out the door, she felt relief flooding through her. From that day on, she and Harry have tried to arrange some time in his schedule at work each week so that he can come home and give Sandy a break. "As hard as it is to find time for yourself and give each other breaks," she says, "we do it regularly now. And it's always a revelation when we do it, how much of a freeing experience it is."

Dad's Point of View

When Bill scheduled a long weekend off for himself to go fishing with two friends, some of his coworkers were critical. Bill was a single father with two sons, 11 and 15, and he planned on leaving them with their grandmother. "I was seen as selfish by some of the people at work because I wanted to take time off away from the kids," he said. "But I knew that if I didn't get a breather, I might start losing my temper at home." Bill was wise enough to realize that he was getting burned out from the continued stress at work and at home, where he was solely responsible for the boys' welfare.

Added to that was the fact that he had no one at home to talk to, and sometimes he just needed to get away for a day or more, so he could come back into the family and take up his responsibilities with new strength.

For Reflection

When was the last time you took a break from your kids?

If you got out your calendar and wrote down a few hours for your own break, would this help or hinder your family life?

Try sitting down and discussing with your partner the importance of occasional breaks from household responsibility.

SET REASONABLE EXPECTATIONS

Set reasonable expectations for creating the kind of family you want. Don't agonize if it doesn't look like a scene from "Leave It to Beaver."

In More Depth

Whether we realize it or not, most of us don't begin our families with a clean slate; we bring along the opinions, expectations, and experiences of our parents, grandparents, and great-grandparents. What makes it even more difficult is that our partner also carries into the marriage a set of preconceived notions of what a family is, how it should act, and how the children should be raised. When two people have different notions—as they almost always have—expectations about how to combine those differences can create real problems. What makes the situation even trickier is that often, these expectations are unconscious. "Doesn't everybody feel this way?" we think.

Expectations about roles, career, housekeeping, and child rearing are all areas that are exquisitely sensitive to interpretation, colored by the lenses of childhood experience.

Mom's Point of View

Jane and her husband Alan are a two-career couple who agree on most areas, including how to raise their three children. They don't fight over who does the housework and they have no problems with money or relationship issues. The stress comes when they "expect" the other to understand traditions developed in their family of origin. Alan, a car salesman, was raised by his mother in a busy household with few rules. Mealtimes at their home had always been haphazard: Brothers and sisters grabbed a bite on the run, and people never sat down together for a meal. Jane, a floral designer, was raised in an extremely rigid, traditional home where dinnertime was a sacred family ritual, with linen tablecloths and the full complement of silver. As a child, Jane can't recall *ever* missing a family dinner for any reason. As long as Jane gets home first and makes the meal, Alan is content to sit down with the family and eat. But if Jane is busy at work—especially over the holidays—she is upset to find that Alan doesn't pick up the slack in her absence.

When it falls to Alan to prepare a meal, he opens a can of soup or throws a sandwich together for the kids while he eats standing up in the kitchen. He prepares nothing for Jane, assuming that she'll make her own meal when she arrives.

Jane realized she needed to sit down and explain to Alan how she feels about traditional meals, and how she resents it when he doesn't pitch in when she isn't able to do so. "A meal isn't just a cheese sandwich or a bowl of tomato soup," she told him. "A meal has vegetables, it has meat or a protein, it has pasta or potatoes or rice. There are placemats on the table—not just folded-up sections of newspaper under the plate. There are napkins and everyone says grace. A meal is an important family time.

"He just didn't get it," she explained. "He didn't see why I was so upset. After it happened many times and each time I got more upset, eventually I blew up."

Dad's Point of View

"Mealtimes just weren't important around my house," Alan says. "I don't do the grocery shopping, and I don't do the meal planning. On those days when Jane can't be here to cook, I'm just trying to find something to feed the kids in a hurry. I just don't have the time to prepare a three-course meal."

Alan and Jane realized they were dealing with alternate expectations. While Jane was raised with the idea that a formal dinner is important to a happy family, Alan wonders who has time to cook a big meal after getting home late and exhausted from a full day's work outside the home. What happens to the plan when one parent gets home much later than the other? Young children often can't wait until 8:00 or 9:00 P.M. Do you have two or three mealtimes to accommodate those schedules? As kids get older, afterschool activities may also interfere with dinnertime.

Alan and Jane reached a compromise: Since mealtimes were important to Jane, she would prepare the elaborate dinners. When it was Alan's turn, Jane accepted that dinner would be more casual. Once the issue was out in the open, they both were able to compromise.

For Reflection

How do your desires and expectations differ from your partner's?

When you find yourself reacting strongly over fairly minor points, look into your background to see if the problem is really based on childhood experiences.

Can you live with the fact that family life will never be perfect because individuals are imperfect? Can you move on and live with the mess?

WHO'S RESPONSIBLE?

The unspoken mantle of responsibility—for the paychecks, for child care, for care of the home—must be shared equally if the two-career family is to function best.

In More Depth

Ideally, in a two-career family the balance of power is shared between both partners so that no one must struggle with an overwhelming load. In fact, however, this is often not the case. Women tend to assume more of the child-care responsibilities in even the most untraditional households. And far too often, men find themselves shouldering the responsibility for the "bottom line"—for making sure the family is financially secure.

Mom's Point of View

Traci is a screenwriter and the mother of two sons who struggles daily with unspoken assumptions about whose job it is to do what. "A lot of the responsibility for kids and the house still falls upon women, no matter how enlightened men think they are," she says. Women often feel as if they have expectations coming at them from all directions: from themselves, loved ones, in-laws, parents and siblings, friends, colleagues—all because of the many roles a woman juggles. "Men have multiple roles too," Traci says, "but society accepts it when they hand off responsibilities or make a mistake. If we do that, we're 'having trouble getting it all done right.' For example, when a man delegates his child-care or home responsibilities—hires a nanny or a cleaning service—he's seen as proactive, but when a woman does this, she's viewed as weak, incapable, or selfish."

Traci also struggles with what she sees as a double standard: "If a man goes to pick up a sick child at school, people will say 'Isn't that nice?' But if his wife leaves *her* job to do the same, it's 'Oops! She's slipping up, is conflicted, has too much to do.' Sometimes women just can't win. The playing field isn't level."

Traci says she knows there's not much she can do about the way society views responsibilities of different genders. What she can do—and does—is to sit down with her husband and talk out her frustration with the inequities. As a result, he's far more sensitive than many men about what true responsibility means.

Dad's Point of View

George is an experienced pilot with an excellent career outlook and two lovely daughters. When his wife's company was recently taken over by another, there was a real concern that she might be out of a job. Although it was his wife's job that was threatened, George felt an unspoken assumption that the financial health of the family was primarily his concern—if they couldn't pay the bills, it would be *his fault*. "My wife never said too much, but she didn't seem that concerned either. I felt like everybody—my parents, my friends, society in general—really believes that when push comes to shove, how well a family does financially is really a man's problem. It drove me crazy."

Indeed, while women often complain that society still expects them to be primary caregivers and housewives even when they hold down full-time jobs, they often forget that society has expectations for men too, however outmoded those beliefs may be. Among these is the idea that a man is the "real" breadwinner who holds ultimate, final responsibility for the financial security of the family. In times when men and women both work, it's unfair to expect a man to be solely responsible for the family's financial health when times get bad.

In George's case, he sat down and talked with his wife about his feelings of stress. "She had no idea how I was feeling," George said. "Once she realized the problem, she admitted she probably assumed that I'd just somehow solve our financial problems. Once she understood how I felt, the pressure seemed much easier to bear right away. In the end, she got to keep her job too, so we were better off all the way around."

For Reflection

Do you and your partner share child-care duties equally? If your child became ill in the middle of the night, which one of you would handle the situation? Who would stay home with the child?

Do you have "hidden responsibilities" around your house—jobs that just "get done" by one or the other partner without discussion? Who handles most of these hidden jobs?

How do you and your partner decide which responsibilities to handle? When was the last time you discussed them?

MAKE A DATE

It may seem artificial, but making a weekly date with your partner can mean all the difference between feeling close and in touch or distant and removed.

In More Depth

Marriage counselors agree that the stress of trying to combine job, home, and child-care responsibilities places an incredible strain on a relationship. One of the most common ways to ease that burden is to set up a weekly (or at least bimonthly) date to get away, catch a movie, or go out to eat. Growing families often have tight budgets, and some couples can find it hard to rationalize spending money on themselves when there are pressing bills. But since it's the *time,* not the expense that counts, you don't have to spend a lot to reap the benefits. If money is short, don't go for an expensive meal—stop at a fast-food place, and take the food to a picnic grove. Pack your own picnic and spread your blanket at a nearby park. Or don't eat at all—just go for a long hike or a romantic stroll by a lake. If you can't afford a babysitter, see if one of your parents or siblings might watch the kids for a couple of hours. Rent a movie and watch it at home, just the two of you. If no family lives nearby, try joining a babysitting co-op, and rotate babysitting duties with friends.

The point is to share some time alone with each other so that you can spend time on your relationship. Doing so will benefit the entire family. Your kids need to see that you value each other and your time spent together, if they are to grow up and establish healthy relationships of their own.

Mom's Point of View

As a psychiatric nurse at a large inpatient facility, Janet was aware of mental-health issues and was an avid reader of parenting articles in the many magazines to which she subscribed. "All the experts comment on the importance of being alone with your spouse as a way of rejuvenating yourselves," she says. "But I just can't make my husband go along."

For the first years of their daughter's life, the two were on a strict budget—so strict that they felt they couldn't justify spending money on babysitters and fun for themselves. But as their daughter moved into preschool age, their financial situation improved markedly. Suddenly, they could well afford a few nights out alone a month—but old habits die hard. Janet's husband was especially reluctant to spend time away from their daughter. He hardly got to see her enough as it was, he told Janet. And he never really trusted anyone else's ability to take care of his daughter.

"I finally realized that if I wanted to go out with my husband, I had to take the initiative," Janet says. She arranged for John's mother to watch their daughter, and made reservations at a local restaurant. When she told John, he hesitated but—since the arrangements had been made—he agreed to go along with them. Once out on the date, he enjoyed himself immensely and admitted that it was nice to be able to sit and talk to Janet for 20 minutes without a preschooler's interruptions.

Since that night, Janet has planned nights out every other week. "I realized it was a compromise, so I didn't push for weekly dates," she says. "I figured John's tolerance was probably just twice a month, at least to start with."

Dad's Point of View

Tom is an airline mechanic whose work requires long, stressful hours away at the airport. His wife Melanie is a full-time English teacher who spends hours each night planning lessons and grading papers. Between Tom's overtime and Melanie's evening work, they don't often get to spend too much time together. They were beginning to feel almost like strangers when Melanie started to push Tom to set up a time each week to go on a date, just the two of them. "I knew that she was right," Tom says, "but it seemed so frivolous. It just seemed less important than getting our work done and spending time with the kids."

Tom also admits that both of them were reluctant to trust a babysitter with their children, and their relatives were not eager to babysit for them. "It always seemed like more of an ordeal than it was worth," Tom says.

Then the two met a teenaged girl who had recently moved into their neighborhood, and they both felt confident about the ability of this young woman to take good care of their kids. "Melanie made reservations at a restaurant only 5 minutes from the house," Tom says, "and so we went. It was really great to get away like that, and we felt like we were close enough if there was a problem."

For Reflection

When was the last time that you and your partner spent a night out alone?

Many parents insist that they have valid reasons for not making a date with their spouse. If this is your case, make a list of all your reasons. Are they really unsolvable?

If finances are a big problem, try making a list of six things you could do with your spouse that cost little or nothing.

COMMUNICATION IS THE KEY

Although the key to any successful relationship is good communication, it's even more important when you're both juggling multiple roles.

In More Depth

The stress of today's working parents is unrelenting and can take many forms: too little time, too little money, too many chores, job pressures, and the never-ending responsibility for raising healthy, happy children. Add to that the stress of changing social roles—bringing many traditional expectations into direct conflict with today's realities—and it's not surprising that many working parents feel sometimes crushing conflicts.

All this stress can strain even the healthiest relationships if there isn't a solid way for working through disagreements. Mental-health experts agree that the ability to sit down and talk honestly with your partner is probably one of the best ways to ensure the success of your relationship.

Mom's Point of View

Unresolved anger is one of the hallmarks of poor couple communication. It was a real problem for Marsha, a beautician, and her husband. Unable to resolve their angry feelings, they simply chose to withdraw from each other. After the children went to bed, they would simply retreat to different parts of the house. Not surprisingly, the anger went underground and continued to fester.

"Finally, I couldn't stand it anymore," Marsha said. "I tracked Alan down and just had it out with him—just sat down and said 'We've got to talk.' After an exhausting 3-hour discussion, they realized that they had let too many fairly minor problems go unresolved, accumulating into a mass of negative feelings.

What they decided to do was schedule a weekly family meeting on Sundays after the kids were in bed. They made up a formal agenda, and every week they discuss whatever's on their minds, while planning for the upcoming week.

"The difference the weekly meeting has made is unbelievable," Marsha says. "Now when there is a problem about chores not getting done or someone feeling slighted, it doesn't have a chance to build up. We know we'll have to talk about it on Sunday." A bonus, they found, was that they both have a much better idea of the family schedule and upcoming potential problems. Alan has a better idea of special events at school that he needs to plan for, and Marsha feels that Alan is more involved than ever in the family.

"Since we both work and we both have to take care of the kids and the house, the weekly meetings have really saved our sanity!"

Dad's Point of View

Lowell is a sales manager for the entire northeast, and his job frequently takes him away from home. When his children were very young, his wife resented the added burden of shouldering child care alone. One day when Lowell was away on business, their 6-year-old son and some of his friends were discovered trespassing in an abandoned building. The baby developed a serious respiratory problem and had to be rushed to the hospital, and the 3-year-old began acting out in day care. As if this wasn't enough, the car's exhaust system failed and the toilet broke down—all on the same day. "It's funny now, but it wasn't funny then," Lowell says. Since neither Lowell nor his wife felt that quitting his lucrative position was the answer, the two of them sat down and discussed their problems rationally. They negotiated personal time on a weekly basis to make up for the hours that Lowell spent away from home, guaranteeing his wife some time on her own.

The best situation is to anticipate possible problems and develop workable solutions. When that's not always feasible, you can still come up with answers after the fact. What Lowell learned is that what's not a good idea is to assume that the problem is just going to go away. It never does.

"Be clear about your needs and make sure the solution is equitable for you and your spouse," Lowell says. "I felt it was only fair to give my wife extra personal time when I had been away. It's important to make the time in your hectic schedule to discuss what's bothering you."

For Reflection

Would you say that you communicate well with your partner? What does your partner say?

How would things change between you and your partner if your communication was improved?

When you find yourself discussing a problem with your partner, does it often escalate into an argument? Can you think of ways to approach the problem in a more constructive way?

WHO STAYS HOME?

When a child is sick, the test of equality in a relationship is often revealed when it comes to deciding who stays home.

In More Depth

In some relationships, the type of career each partner has often dictates who will stay home when the children are sick. If one parent works at home and the other has a strictly scheduled shift, it's fairly clear who will inherit sickroom duty. In other families, an unequal balance of power means that it's almost always the woman who remains behind to care for an ailing child.

In most situations, however, the decision about who will care for a sick child is stressful because *neither* parent can really afford the time off. How do parents cope when there's no easy way to decide who will stay home?

The answer, many social scientists say, is that in America there should be a recognition on the corporate level that families need support. Employers need to be better able to cope with flexible child-care arrangements and more willing to understand that an employee who is not stressed out because of family concerns will be a better, more loyal worker. Until that day comes, working couples will simply need to share the load.

Mom's Point of View

Yvonne is a corporate communications director for a large metropolitan real estate company, with a 4-year-old son and a 2-year-old daughter. If one of the children is sick, Yvonne and her husband, an engineer with a fairly flexible schedule, compare schedules and decide to split sick days or alternate, if necessary. "My company is actually male-oriented and quite traditional," Yvonne says, "but it has been flexible with me." Her company's vice president of human resources, a male, has been very supportive and actively looks into flexible schedules that work for everyone.

In addition, Yvonne is lucky enough to live near a nursing school, and occasionally she hires a nursing student to come to her home and watch her children. Because of her nursing training, Yvonne feels comfortable having the sitter give her son his asthma medicine or breathing treatments, if necessary. Yvonne also makes use of a local hospital which charges $35 per day for "sick-child care." The hospital requires only documentation of current immunizations.

Dad's Point of View

Sam is a midlevel manager at a nonprofit association who has just moved into a new position at his company, with higher salary and potential for advancement. For this reason, he tends to be the one who works and his wife is the one who most often stays at home when necessary. "I would love to make the switch at some point," he says, "and be the primary caretaker so our kids don't grow up thinking only moms stay at home and take care of kids. People can do different things and kids shouldn't be hemmed in by role models."

For the moment, however, it just doesn't seem feasible. And while Sam's wife agrees, Sam says she also admits to feeling resentful sometimes for having to deal with the bulk of emergency child care.

For Reflection

If your child wakes up sick this morning, will one of you automatically be the parent who stays home?

If you feel resentful about bearing the burden of sick-child duty, what other plan could you come up with to share the burden more equally?

How would you feel about finding other alternatives to caring for a sick child, such as hospital-based "sick child" day care or nursing school students for at-home babysitting?

LOWER YOUR STANDARDS

Chances are the world won't end if your floors are dirty and the laundry sits unfolded in the basket.

In More Depth

When there are an infinite number of jobs and only a few hours in which to get them accomplished, something has to give. What many working parents have discovered is that it's far better to have a pile of dirty clothes and a sinkful of dishes than an unhappy, neglected child.

Many working parents today were raised with the ethos of the 1950s, in which a sparkling home was considered to be essential for a happy family life. But this was possible only because women stayed at home all day to wipe down the bathroom walls and wax the kitchen floors.

The problem is that too many of us carry some portion of this 1950s mentality into the 1990s reality. "I remember my mother washing the woodwork and ironing the tea towels," says one working mom. "She even ironed my father's undershorts. Her house *sparkled*—but that was her job. That was *all* she was expected to do."

Mom's Point of View

The best advice that Sue Ellen says she ever got was to lower her housekeeping standards in favor of spending time with her child. "I have to clean up at some point, but when things get hectic I dump housework first," she says.

A single mom with one son, Sue is a part-time attorney who faces a long commute each day to her large downtown firm. Separated from her husband, mother and son live on her part-time salary and do almost everything together, including running errands and shopping. "Sharing the routine is a good way to teach life skills and practice things like math," she says.

Dad's Point of View

Dan is a midlevel manager in a building products company who says he is frustrated by the issue of household chores. He and his wife both hold down demanding, full-time jobs while raising their two boys, ages 7 and 10. "I don't feel like we're equal when it comes to the chores around the house," he says, "because my wife acts like the mom and treats me like the little kid." His wife criticizes him for everything he tries to do around the house. "She doesn't like the way I vacuum. She says I shrink her clothes when I do the laundry. She doesn't like the brands I buy at the store."

Moreover, Dan is much more laid back when it comes to how clean he thinks the house needs to be. His wife, he says, insists the floors must be shining and the cupboards immaculate. He'd rather be playing with his boys. He admits he takes a more laissez-faire attitude with housecleaning.

"I think women say they don't want to have to do it all, but they really have a hard time letting go and allowing their husbands to do jobs a different way." In the end, Dan and his wife reached a compromise that many working parents find helpful—they simply hired a cleaning woman who comes in twice a week to do the jobs they can't agree on. "It's more than worth the money," Dan says. "You have to take into consideration the aggravation factor. Fighting about chores just isn't worth it."

For Reflection

How many times in the last week did you fail to meet your own standards of perfection at home and on the job?

What would the consequences be if you failed to complete all your household tasks in favor of playing with your kids?

In 10 years, will you or the kids remember if you washed the kitchen walls?

APPRECIATE EACH OTHER

A kind word after a rough day at work can do wonders for bolstering our inner resources.

In More Depth

The boss hates your presentation. The car exhaust is rumbling ominously and as you come up your driveway, you notice the porch needs to be painted. The kids are fighting in the back seat and the youngest brings home a "D" on her report card. Sometimes what makes the difference between blowing up and cooling off are the kind, appreciative words from our partner—or our children.

"I know you must have had a rough day at work," one husband observed as his harried wife staggered in the door. "Why don't you lie down on the sofa and I'll get dinner?"

Whenever we take the time to notice the efforts of our partner or our kids, we're saying, "I've noticed your sacrifice." At a time when both partners are usually stretched to the limit, a simple "thank you" can make all the difference between resentment and relief.

Mom's Point of View

One of the jobs that often fell to Moira, a self-employed computer company employee, was of ferrying their daughter Karen to birthday parties. Because they lived far away from most of Karen's friends, this usually meant the loss of quite a chunk of a weekend afternoon. Moira took on the job of chauffeur because her husband felt uncomfortable at birthday parties in the midst of a sea of mothers and daughters.

One sunny Saturday afternoon, Moira was bogged down in work and her husband offered to take Karen to the party—an hour's drive from their home. Moira knew that her husband had lined up a long list of jobs he dearly wanted to finish, and that he had planned on stopping by the lumber yard to pick up some items.

"When he came home, I gave him a hug and told him how much I appreciated his taking over that job for me so I could work," she says. "He kind of shrugged it off as nothing much, but I could see he was pleased. He had really put aside all his plans for things he wanted to do so that I could work, and I wanted to make sure he knew I valued his sacrifice."

Dad's Point of View

"I was having a really rough week at work," Stan says. "None of the customers seemed to be satisfied and my boss was being demanding and unfair." Traffic was snarled and the temperature was oppressively humid. By the time Stan got home that night, he was in a foul temper.

When he walked in the door, he threw his briefcase on the floor and caught his 6-year-old daughter in a hug. His daughter begged Stan to come out and play ball—the last thing Stan felt like doing at the time.

"But I looked in her little face, and how could I say no?" asked Stan, whose own father had had little time for him. "Oh, thank you!" she told him. "You're the best daddy in the whole world!"

The disappointment of the week fell away like magic. "All of a sudden, nothing mattered anymore," Stan recalled. "That one sentence of appreciation took away all my weariness, anger, and bad feelings."

For Reflection

How many times have you told your partner or your children that you appreciated something they did for you?

Compare this with how much time you've spent criticizing them.

Think of five nice things your partner has done for you lately. Did you acknowledge any of them? If not, what would your spouse say if you wrote a brief note today?

LEARN TO COMPROMISE

Job, home, and child responsibilities take up so much of our time. Don't waste time fighting over incidentals.

In More Depth

More often than not, working couples arrive home tired, hot, irritated, and stretched to the breaking point. In an atmosphere like this, it's easy to see how minor annoyances can blow up into big fights.

She forgot to turn off the heater in the morning. *He* left the milk out on the counter. *She* never closes doors or drawers. *He* leaves his underwear behind the bathroom door.

What is a small annoyance to one person can be a major problem to another, in part because of the way we have been brought up. If cleanliness was next to godliness to your mom and dad, then leaving the toothpaste cap off may seem like high treason to you.

The key to living in peace when you're stretched to the limit is to ask yourself whether each incident *really matters* to anyone but you. If the answer is no, can you manage to overlook it? Ask yourself if it's going to be important in 10 years, and act accordingly.

Mom's Point of View

When it came to cleaning, the only thing that Anne and Colin fought about was the bathroom. "He will vacuum without being asked," Anne says of her husband, "but he will not clean the bathroom. He came right out and said it one day: 'I will not clean the bathroom.'"

In Anne's opinion, the logical solution was to alternate vacuuming and bathroom cleaning. After all, she says, "I always do laundry and I always pick up." But still Colin adamantly refused.

"So," Anne says, "I thought: 'Fine. I'm not doing it.'" She waited to see what happened—but when nothing happened, she was nonplussed. "Considering bathrooms of his that I've seen in the past, I don't think he would care if it never got done."

Anne eventually realized that, however illogical, this was one battle she was not going to win. Since Colin willingly shared every other household duty and was an excellent father to their daughter Molly, Anne decided it just wasn't a serious enough problem to keep fighting about. He agreed to vacuum permanently, and she's been cleaning the bathroom ever since.

Dad's Point of View

Weekday mornings can be rough when everyone is in a hurry to get ready for work and school. It was a particular problem at Mark's house, because the family had only one bathroom.

"My wife takes forever in there, especially on mornings when she showers first," Mark said. "We all have to leave at the same time, and we have to pack our daughter's lunch, and get her dressed and ready too." They all had to get up at 6:00 A.M., and it wasn't really possible for any of them to get up any earlier than that. Mark finally sat down and discussed the problem with his wife, and the two of them came up with a compromise: Since Mark took less time in the bathroom than his wife, he could go first at a scheduled time. While he was in the bathroom, his wife would lay out their daughter's clothes, brush her hair, and organize her school bag.

When it was his wife's turn, Mark would pack his daughter's lunch and supervise her dressing. They would set up the coffee maker the night before so that neither of them had to fuss with making coffee.

"It may sound like a minor solution, but to us it really saved frazzled nerves and flaring tempers," Mark says.

For Reflection

How many times in the past month have you lost your temper over a minor irritation?

Keep in mind that a compromise means you both lose something, but you also both win something. How well do you handle compromise?

When you fight, are you trying to solve problems or win an argument at all costs?

Working at Home

JUST SAY NO

Just because you work at home doesn't mean you have to be a doormat.

In More Depth

Parents who work at home say the situation seems to carry a whole host of psychological baggage—no one seems to believe you're really working at a job. Self-employed parents commonly report that people will ask them when they are going to "get a job." Friends and family members think that since you're not working for a company and your time is your own, and you'll always have spare moments to run errands for them or chat on the phone.

Being able to work for yourself while raising a family has benefits, but it also carries certain responsibilities. You must be disciplined enough to work hard without supervision, in the presence of a host of attractive distractions. It also means you've got to be able to explain to others that being self-employed doesn't mean you work only when you feel like it. It means you work hard, every day.

When people call to chat, explain you can't talk on company time. When others ask you to do errands, be firm in turning down the requests. This can be especially difficult when it's your own partner who's doing the asking, but it's just as important that your spouse respect your work-life parameters as anyone else. Of course, this means you have to take yourself seriously as a self-employed worker, or no one else will.

Mom's Point of View

Anne was a freelance editorial consultant who worked out of a home office and raised her daughter, age 4. She had become fairly adept at fitting in her work during times when her daughter was occupied, attending preschool, or visiting with friends.

The problem was that because she worked at home, no one really believed she was working. Friends would call on the phone; relatives would drop by for visits. Other relatives were constantly calling her up to ask her to run an errand as a favor. "Could you take the cat to the vet for me?" asked her mother, who lived next door. "I'm on a deadline," she replied. "But can't you just run the cat up to the vet?" her mother repeated, as if she hadn't heard. "Mother, I'm *working*," Anne repeated, a little louder. Sometimes friends would stop by and say, "Oh, are you busy?"

Anne finally had to learn to put her foot down. She refused all requests from family members to run errands during working hours, no matter how innocuous they seemed. She would lock the front door and lower the blinds to discourage drop-in visits, and when friends would call and ask if she was busy, she steeled herself to say "Yes, I am."

Dad's Point of View

Jim was a self-employed marketing consultant who worked out of his home office while taking care of a daughter, 6, and son, 4. He also had a problem with family members not understanding the pressures and requirements of his job. In his case, one of the worst offenders was his wife, a factory worker who could not leave the building during working hours.

"Candy didn't have the time to run those annoying errands during the day that lots of people take care of during lunch hour," Jim said, "and she would expect me to do them. It got to be a real pain; she'd want me to run out and pick up her dry cleaning, shop at the store, buy stamps, and mail packages for her."

It wasn't that Jim minded helping out or sharing jobs equally around the house, he says. Many of his wife's requests for him to do errands showed that she expected him to accomplish the tasks during the day, "since you're home." The implication was that he wasn't really working, and she was, so he got stuck with the errands.

"For a while I just went ahead and did the errands, but it got to be too much," Jim says. "I was spending all my time running to the bank, the post office, the hardware store, the dry cleaner." Since he was also juggling child care and lining up sitters to care for their kids, he found that he had to spend more and more time working at night to make up for the time he lost during the day. He realized something needed to be done.

"I sat down with Candy and showed her a list of jobs that I'd done the week before," he says. "She was astonished at the amount of time I'd been spending on these jobs that she had taken for granted." Many of the errands weren't pressing, and could be handled on the weekends when they both had more time. Jim assured Candy he had no problem in taking care of emergencies, but really needed to spend work time at home doing work, not other tasks. "Once Candy saw what had been happening, she felt bad that she'd been taking advantage of my situation."

For Reflection

How many times during the last week did you run errands that had nothing to do with your job?

Keep a log of personal phone call time during office hours. Are you spending too much time chatting with friends instead of getting the job done?

Make a list of common interruptions that happen during the day. Look over each one and ask yourself how you could have avoided getting involved.

SET UP SYSTEMS

Parents who work at home often grapple with unique kinds of problems. By setting up systems to deal with these special problems, you can ease the stress of your at-home situation.

In More Depth

It never fails: Just when that important new business client is on the phone ready to talk, the 2-year-old wakes up from her nap and the baby's colic kicks in. How can you sound businesslike and professional with children crying in the background, *Mr. Rogers* blaring from the TV, and the dog whining at your feet?

While being self-employed and working at home seems like an idyllic dream to most parents, those who actually live and work from the same address know better. "There's very little 'work' involved when you're trying to take care of kids at the same time," one veteran of the home-based business world explains. "It's kind of like people who think it would be fun to run a restaurant or bookstore," another commented. "It seems easy and fun until you actually experience what it's like."

Even seasoned parents tend to gush when contemplating how wonderful it must be to "be able to work and raise your kids at the same time." What these parents don't realize is that when you live over the store, nothing gets done without lots of organization, planning, and a very good system.

Mom's Point of View

Annie is a gifted medical artist who quit a prestigious job with a large medical center in order to work at home and raise her son. By the time he was 4, she felt he should be old enough to play by himself at least for short periods of time. But Annie was having trouble making this system work.

"It was impossible to sit down for 10 minutes at a time and get anything done. When I was at my drafting table, he'd come over wanting a drink, asking for paper, wanting me to turn on a video." When Steve's preschool ended for the summer, Annie realized that something had to be done or she wouldn't be able to meet an important deadline to illustrate a medical textbook.

"I realized Steve's constant stream of requests was really a bid for my attention," she says. "He didn't really need three drinks of water in 15 minutes. I realized it must be hard for him to share his mom."

Annie set up a system of play times and work times. Each hour that he could amuse himself, he would earn an hour of one-on-one time with mom. Because an hour can be hard for a 4-year-old to conceptualize, Annie set a timer for this period so that Steve could check for himself how fast time was passing. At the start of each "play time" hour, Annie made sure there were plenty of materials to keep Steve busy: books, art materials, puzzles, and games. Most of the time, she didn't have to resort to a video.

"It worked like a charm," Annie says. "And since he knew I'd be playing with him soon, he didn't need to keep interrupting me. He was happy to play, knowing that soon we'd be doing something fun together."

Dad's Point of View

While anyone trying to combine parenting with at-home work finds it tough, the pressures are particularly hard for parents of multiples. Kyle is the father of twins who balances his child-care efforts with his own medical transcription service. "If you're a parent of twins, you need to make sure you have some type of system," he says, "or you'll go crazy. And trying to work from home while raising them is even more difficult." Kyle makes sure the babies maintain the same nap times and bedtimes. When it's time for a story, he sits between the cribs and reads to both at the same time.

A babysitter comes in to spell Kyle during the day, and at 2:00 P.M. he begins a cycle of playing, feeding, and outdoor exercise. Kyle and his wife realized while the babies were still in the hospital that the only way they could make it work was if they came up with systems of organization for laundry, housecleaning, grocery shopping, and food preparation. By keeping things on the same time schedule each day, Kyle always knows when he can make business arrangements and when he has some time free.

For Reflection

Are there days when you feel like you're falling behind in work and in chores at home, and you still never get to have quality time with the kids?

Pick one area of your life to focus on. What sort of system could you come up with to streamline your day?

Are you resisting the idea of a system because it feels like a rut?

GOOD FENCES MAKE GOOD PARTNERS

When you both work from home, there's a real risk of too much togetherness. Physically separating your offices can make good sense.

In More Depth

Parents who must work on the outside often fantasize about how wonderful it would be to be able to work from home. Computer message boards are filled with notes from men and women seeking ideas for how to earn money while staying home, enabling them to "be there" for their youngsters.

When both partners have the luxury of working from the home, there are real benefits: more time with the children, greater flexibility for school events and errands, and financial gain from savings in gas, wardrobe, parking, and lunches out. But according to couples who have done it, too much togetherness can be a bad thing.

Endless proximity can lead to petty arguments and a lack of growth in the relationship. When the only adults you see are each other, after a while you may notice a lack of freshness or outright boredom start to creep in. The biggest problem, it seems, is when two partners try to share an office. When every transaction, every telephone call, and every moment is shared, the enforced closeness can be cloying.

If you must work at home, it's a good idea to at least separate your work areas so that you share some private space. This is particularly important when two of you have different opinions about neatness and organization.

Mom's Point of View

Fiona and her husband Ted both work for Ted's father's telecommunications company from their large, spacious home. Parents of three daughters, they spend almost all their time together, since they don't have separate offices to go to during the day. Two of their three daughters are still at home, and require lots of personal attention during the day.

"I love my husband very much," Fiona says, "but frankly, we were getting on each other's nerves." As time went on, they found themselves bickering over little things. Fiona was neat and Ted was not, and she would get upset when she had to find something on his messy desk. Since they shared an office, his messy environment got on Fiona's nerves. When Fiona would take social calls on the phone, Ted would get annoyed. It got to the point where they would work all day side by side in an atmosphere of tense silence.

Fortunately, at about this time they moved into a much larger house, and Fiona broached the subject of setting up separate offices. They had always worked out of the same space, but Ted agreed that they seemed to be getting on each other's nerves. On the third floor were twin rooms with a communicating space in between. Each partner took one room, and they placed the copy and fax machines in a central location. Now that they had some physical space, Ted didn't feel obligated to keep his desk the way Fiona liked it, which had always irked him. Fiona was free to chat on the phone occasionally with friends without feeling like Ted was listening in anger. Fiona was able to close her eyes to Ted's mess, and she was able to decorate her space the way she liked.

"The two separate spaces make all the difference in the world," she says. "It also means that the kids can come in and play with one of us while the other works in peace. That's a big plus, too."

Dad's Point of View

Neil just took a new job as computer consultant for a pharmaceutical firm in another state. Unwilling to move, Neil reached an agreement with the firm to set up a home office and commute a few days a month. He had assumed he could simply move his desk into his wife's home office—but his wife had another view altogether.

"Since April already had her office just the way she liked it," Neil says, "she resented my entering what she felt was 'her' territory. To me, it was just a room we were sharing. But to her it was a whole way of life."

Everyone has a sense of personal physical boundaries. In April's case, her office was her own personal space and Neil was violating those boundaries. She had set up her life in a comfortable way, including the part-time care of their son, who also spent time in a good daycare center near home. "She told me that her whole routine was going to be different now that I was at home and having me on top of her was just too much," Neil said. "We sat down and realized that the only way this was going to work was if I set up my office in a totally different part of the house."

For Reflection

How do you and your partner feel about your office—is it just somewhere to put your computer, or do you have a real personal need for private space?

When you are both in the home office together, do you alter your behavior or your phone conversation as a result? How does that make you feel?

What would happen if one of you moved your home office to another part of the house, or even rented office space elsewhere? Would that make your jobs easier or harder?

INVEST IN TECHNOLOGY

If you're going to work from home, make full use of all that modern technology has to offer you to make the job easier.

In More Depth

If you've been working from your home for some time, you may not have realized that the explosion of technology has revolutionized the home office to the point where you don't have to be tethered to your office to get work done.

Laptops, e-mail, and telecommunication have really done a lot for moms and dads who want to spend more time at home with their families but still hang onto their jobs.

Mom's Point of View

Taking advantage of the most up-to-date telecommuting possibilities made all the difference for Terri, who holds an MBA from an Ivy League school and struggled for years up the corporate ladder before having a baby. "My 12-month-old has changed my perspective of the career track," she says. Although she still works a 60-hour week, she was able to set up a schedule with her bosses to allow her to work from home one day a week using a special computer program that gave her access to her computer at home.

When she's at home connected to work via computer, she also takes calls from the office and from clients while spending quality time with her son. She knows that men in her office now consider her to be less productive and less career-oriented. "But I think I have shown them that it's possible to balance both home and career," she says.

Dad's Point of View

Jim was a freelance indexer who was constantly faced with the challenge of working at home, balancing child care and job responsibilities. While his family and friends would often call during working hours, he was especially bothered by nuisance "cold" calls by salespeople and solicitors. One day, after he was interrupted on five separate occasions by computerized dialing machines, he began letting his answering machine screen all his calls.

At first, his friends and family didn't like the system. When he would pick up after letting the answering machine take the call, they would ask "Are you screening your calls?" with thinly veiled hostility. Calmly, Jim would explain that he couldn't afford a secretary, so the machine was the second-best thing. Eventually, they all learned to accept the machine as part of the way he had to do business.

"I couldn't believe how much time it saved when I stopped answering my phone," he says. "And I couldn't believe how angry it seemed to make people when they realized I was screening my calls. I had to get over feeling defensive, because it was the only way I could get work done."

For Reflection

Think about ways you could tap into modern technology to free yourself to spend more time at home, more productively.

Make a list of your current job responsibilities. Are there ways that you could use new types of office equipment to make that job easier? These could include:

- *New on-line computer services*
- *Innovative phone-billing services to separate work and home calls*
- *New telecommuting capabilities with extra-fast telephone connections*
- *Answering machines and computerized answering machine capability*
- *Phone services such as call waiting, caller ID, and call forwarding*

It's easy to get complacent about advances in office systems. Make a list of ways you can get more up to date on what's available—through one-day workshops, magazines, networking, and so on.

REACH OUT

Working at home and taking care of children at the same time can be a lonely, isolating experience. Reach out to others in your situation to ease the burden of loneliness.

In More Depth

To many working parents, the possibility of working out of their home while simultaneously taking care of children seems like the best of all worlds. How wonderful, it seems, to be able to stay at home, earn money, and be with your kids, all at the same time!

As with all dreams, the reality of this one is not quite as rosy as it might seem. And what surprises work-at-home parents even more is that the experience can be emotionally draining. There's little time for interacting with other parents, and there is no interaction with colleagues at an office.

Mom's Point of View

Sarah, a self-employed travel agent, was delighted at first at being able to combine her career with raising her young son Nicky. But after 3 years of trying to juggle her job at home and her son's care, she became disillusioned.

"I found the isolation really difficult to deal with," she says. "All my contacts—friends and former coworkers—were working full time. There was no one here to talk to except Nicky. Of course I love him, but he's only 3! I needed an adult once in a while for a sanity check."

Eventually, Sarah realized she needed to start reaching out and become connected with the women on her street who stayed at home. After all, when she worked in the agency, her friends were those in nearby offices. Now that she was at home, she needed to look around her for stimulation. "At first it was kind of hard, because I felt the other moms resented me for being able to have a job and stay at home. But I also think part of that was in my own head."

Sarah started by inviting two women from her street over for brunch one day. While their children entertained themselves, she was able to get to know the two women a bit better, and found that they all had more in common than she had realized. One of the women had been an art history major in college, and loved visiting art museums—Sarah's favorite activity. They made a date for the following week to take in a new exhibit with their two children. From there, Sarah found it was much easier to reach out to other women on her street.

Dad's Point of View

Bill is a self-employed medical writer for a pharmaceuticals firm who combines his job with taking care of his 5-year-old daughter Emily. "I've heard self-employed moms say they get lonely, but that's nothing to what I've experienced," Bill says. His male colleagues say they envy him, but all too often they will ask him when he's coming "back to work," implying that his present job doesn't really count. "I kind of feel out of the loop with my friends who work in offices," he says, "but it's impossible to reach out to the women who live nearby." Bill is the only work-at-home dad, and there are no other males for him to meet during the day where he lives. But the women on his street seem reluctant to include him. "Now I know how women feel when they're excluded from men's clubs," he says. "I feel I'm not welcome at the park or the zoo. And forget play groups!"

Bill had despaired of ever connecting with adults during the day until he happened to find some notes from other men in similar situations on a popular on-line computer message board. Since he lived in a large city, he was surprised to discover others like himself who lived in the vicinity and who had likewise been struggling with isolation. Just leaving messages for each other felt enormously supportive. Eventually, several of the men and their kids got together for a picnic at a local park. They've been meeting ever since.

For Reflection

How many times in the last month did you get together during the day with another person besides your own child?

Make a list of at least three ways to meet others who work at home while taking care of kids.

Make a list of five community organizations you could join or volunteer activities you could do that would allow you to include your children while also meeting new adults.

SCHEDULE YOUR TIME

By altering your hours to fit in with your family's schedule, you can avoid some direct conflicts.

In More Depth

When you're busy juggling work, home, and child care, it's easy to fall into predictable routines that all too soon harden into inevitability. Before we know it, we're in a rut and we can't see our way out. This can really become a problem if conflicts arise between our family's needs and our schedules.

When we're in a rut or a routine, it can be hard to see beyond the path of least resistance—the way "I've always done things"—into the uncharted waters of innovative thinking. But that's precisely where we need to go if our old way of doing things isn't working anymore.

The sign of a truly creative mind is the ability to look at problems in unusual ways, from different angles and perspectives. If you're having problems with your schedule, try looking at the problem from a variety of ways. What could you be doing differently?

Mom's Point of View

As Debbie's two girls entered elementary school, she quit her at-home day-care service to start selling beauty products out of her home. Although she liked her new flexibility and independence, she found that her selling job brought a fresh batch of problems. The best time to reach her working-women customers by phone was during the late afternoon and early evening. But this conflicted with the needs of her girls, ages 10 and 13. "They would constantly come to me saying, 'Mom, I need help with my homework. Mom, I need to use the phone,'" Debbie explains.

Her husband wasn't much help. At night he'd become engrossed in TV and ignore Debbie's request that he make sure the girls were in bed on time. As a result, they wouldn't get to sleep until late, and then they couldn't get up for school the next morning.

"It was all on me," Debbie complained. When she realized the problem wasn't going to go away, she decided what needed to be changed was her own schedule. Now she waits to make calls until the girls are on their way to bed. Her bookkeeping gets done after that, when it's too late to make calls and both girls are asleep. Her work gets done on time and she doesn't have to get into fights with her husband about what is or isn't being accomplished with the girls.

"In the best of worlds, he'd help more," she says. "But since I can't seem to win that particular argument, I have to do what works for me."

Dad's Point of View

James is a human resources assistant director for an international building products company. He loves his job and his children, but is deeply upset with his school district for scheduling events during times when he can't attend.

"They schedule special events and even parent report card meetings during the day, with no evening options," he complains. "It appears most of the moms in the class are homemakers and the fathers don't seem to care about not being there." James worries that his children will think he doesn't care enough to come to these special events. "When my kids are sick, when there's a school play, it hurts not being there," he says. "Then when I can't make these events, I feel even worse when the at-home moms smugly imply they are better parents. And the school just doesn't seem to understand that a dad might want to come to these functions." James is especially upset because he feels he's regarded as "odd" for even wanting to attend functions that traditionally have been run and attended by moms.

Eventually, when he realized the school would not change its policy, he revised his schedule so that he could take advantage of flexible afternoon scheduling. On days when a special event is planned at school, he comes in 2 or 3 hours early and then leaves at lunch.

"I'm usually one of the only dads sitting there in the audience," he says, "but I don't care. It's worth it to me when my kids know that I've made the effort to come to school."

For Reflection

If you find that your schedule doesn't mesh with your family's needs, think of innovative ways to break out of the rut.

When was the last time you deviated from your habitual way of doing things and struck out into new territory?

If your schedule isn't working, think of ways you could add time to the day. Start with 15-minute segments. Could you get up earlier? Go to bed later? Find a quicker way to work? Hire someone to do chores you're doing yourself?

Single Parents

ORGANIZE YOUR DAY

Organizing your life can go a long way toward helping you juggle the responsibilities of job, home, and child care, especially when you're playing the roles of mom and dad.

In More Depth

Your briefcase is stocked with papers for the important financial session this afternoon, and there are a stack of bills to be paid on the table. Your son reminds you he needs to be picked up after football practice, and your daughter has a piano lesson to attend. There's a stack of clothes to take to the dry cleaner, an insurance form to fill out, and a birthday present to be mailed to your sister in Iowa. You need to schedule a visit from the water softener man, the stove isn't working right, and the cat has to go to the vet for shots.

Without a plan, odds are some of these important jobs just won't get done.

If the life of working parents is complicated, the life of a *single* working parent is even worse. There's no one else to pick up the slack when your child has to be driven, doctored, or disciplined. There's no one else to call for repairs, schedule meetings, mail birthday cards, and whip up a cake for the school's bake sale. It's all on your shoulders, and without an organization plan, the stress can be completely overwhelming.

Mom's Point of View

"Making lists and sticking to them really does work," says Helen, a midwestern writer currently separated from her husband. "If you aren't organized, it's easy to fall way behind."

When Helen first separated from her husband, the emotional stress from the split plus her daughter's heartbreak were difficult to handle. What made everything worse was that suddenly the whole responsibility for running the household smoothly fell on her shoulders. "This may sound silly," she says, "but there were so many little, stupid things he did that I took for granted. Like he always fed the cat and the dog, made my daughter's sandwich in the morning, and rotated the tires." All of a sudden, the reality of her burdens threatened to overwhelm her.

When Helen missed an important meeting because she'd forgotten to write it down on her calendar, and then got dunning calls when she neglected to mail the gas bill, she realized something had to be done. She got a large calendar for the kitchen, and another small one for her purse to write down every important date. She'd write down messages in advance, reminding herself to check the oil, put on the snow tires, and even turn the clocks back. Every appointment for her daughter got added in the calendar. She also began a daily "to do" list, crossing off each item after it was accomplished. "Not only does it help me stay organized, but I get a real feeling of accomplishment when I can cross off the next duty."

She has lists of necessary grocery items, upcoming gifts to buy, and jobs to accomplish the next day at work. Since she's started her organization program, Helen hasn't missed a meeting or overlooked a household job. "Lists work to keep you focused on job and household responsibilities, commitments to the kids, time for yourself, and even the budget, if you must rein in finances."

Dad's Point of View

William is a newly divorced engineer who shares custody for his 6-year-old son. One of the hardest things he first encountered as a working single parent was trying to get everything done without forgetting important dates and tasks. Although he considers himself to be a perfectionist, his wife was the one who actually took care of many of their social responsibilities and William had gotten used to this luxury.

Without William having to think about it, birthday cards got mailed, vacations were planned, visits were scheduled. It was William's wife who kept track of invitations they received and invitations to which they needed to reciprocate. It had never been William who scheduled pediatric visits, set up play dates, and organized the closets.

In a daze after his divorce, William was bewildered by the chaos around him. He had been married right out of college and never really managed these homely daily details by himself. "I always had such an orderly life," he says. "After the divorce, my life just fell to pieces. Nothing was getting done and I was incredibly depressed about it."

Eventually, his innate sense of order drove him to sit down and devise a plan to take care of the contingencies. Things were complicated by the fact that he and his wife shared custody of their young son. They needed to be in constant communication so as not to duplicate plans for the boy.

With the aid of calendars, checklists, and a small portable dictating machine to give himself reminders, William was able to set up a system of reminders so that nothing was left to chance and hence forgotten. "Once I'd gotten organized, I couldn't believe the difference in my mental outlook," he says. "Once things were predictable, I was much more equipped to handle them."

For Reflection

In the past month, how many important meetings, dates, or appointments have you missed or forgotten?

What would happen if right now you sat down and made lists of all the upcoming dates and appointments you must remember?

Imagine how it would feel if you always knew exactly where you had to go, when you had to be there, and what you needed to bring along when you went. Is this a freeing or a constricting feeling?

DO SOMETHING FOR *YOU*

It may seem selfish, but it will be easier to maintain a healthy outlook at home and work if you have interests in life besides your children.

In More Depth

One of the biggest problems in being a single working parent is that there is so little time and so many things to do. Worst of all, there's no one to pick up the slack: no one to watch the kids while you take a shower, no one to stay home with a sick child when you have an important meeting, no one to shovel the sidewalk, fix the carburetor, or clip the cat's claws.

Given all of this, it's still important that you keep some free time as one of your priorities. No matter how wonderful a parent you are, you simply can't satisfy every demand that is brought to you—and if you try, eventually you will burn out.

It's imperative that you learn to recognize your limitations and once in a while—no matter how guilty this makes you feel—do something, sinfully, just for you. It doesn't mean you need to go overboard: Spend time with friends, read a book, take a long bath. This will teach your children that other people besides themselves have needs, and that taking care of yourself is important. And you'll find that coming back to your kids and your job after a little break makes you a healthier, calmer, happier person.

Mom's Point of View

Sometimes you'll have to take time for yourself no matter what other people say. Their disapproval may hurt, but in the end you're the one who must deal with the stress of working and home life. That's the case for Ariel, a young divorced administrative assistant with twin preschoolers. After the divorce, she began dropping the twins off at her parents' farm for a weekend every month or so.

"I know that some of my friends think I'm awful because I want a bit of time to myself," she says. "They think I'm abandoning my kids. But I realized that there was no way I could handle two active preschoolers on my own without cracking up."

When her parents have the twins, Ariel may go stay with a single girlfriend in a nearby town, watching rented movies and giggling. "It's kind of like a slumber party," she says. "It's just so much fun to be able to talk to another adult and not have to worry about getting up three times in the middle of the night."

Ariel finds that she is far more calm after one of these weekends apart and better able to cope with the twins, and her parents also appreciate the time they can spend alone with their grandchildren. "I try to schedule a weekend about every 6 weeks," she says. "I find that when things get rough, having something to look forward to really helps me cope."

Dad's Point of View

Aaron has sole custody of two girls and a boy, and one of his ironclad rules is that they have to be in bed by 8:30 P.M. "Sometimes I feel badly about having them go to bed so early," he says, "but I have to do it because that's about my limit of tolerance." Aaron works a high-pressure job all day, and finds that the unrelenting pressure of home, job, and child responsibilities often leaves him tense and ready to snap by the end of the day. "I'm afraid if they stayed up any later, little things they did would push me over the edge."

Aaron has realized that he desperately needs those few hours of calm at the end of the day in order to recharge his batteries for the next day's round of problems.

"Sometimes all I do is sit in front of the TV or go for a long walk at night," he says. "But it's enough."

For Reflection

When was the last time that you did something just for you?

What if your parents live too far away and you don't want to impose on friends? Try a co-op: Take a friend's kids for the weekend so he or she can get away, and then reverse the favor the next week.

Realize that if you take time off away from your kids, someone may find fault with you. Can you trust your own judgment rather than someone else's criticism?

YOU DON'T HAVE TO BE A SUPERPARENT

There's no way you can juggle work, home, and kids singlehandedly, and do it all perfectly. Fortunately, your kids don't need perfection—they just need love.

In More Depth

Many single working parents feel pressure to be both mom and dad for their kids, and because there is often lots of guilt in the mix, the pressure to be perfect can feel overwhelming. But when you add job stress, lack of adult companionship, constant responsibility, and full burden for home chores to the list, the result can be almost overwhelming.

In fact, these are the very emotions that many working single parents report. Whether or not the decision to become single parents was theirs, many working parents in this situation feel guilty because their kids don't have a traditional, two-parent family. In an effort to compensate, many try too hard to be perfect. In fact, it's just not possible to be both mother and father to your kids. All you can do is be the best mom or dad you know how to be.

Mom's Point of View

Other single working parents don't even try to combine both jobs. "I've never tried to be both a mom and a dad," says Karen, a military supply clerk. "I guess my goal has always been to be the best mom I could be while balancing my job with parenting skills." Karen sends the kids to her ex-husband for a month in the summer. The rest of the time she keeps them with her on the base, where they are involved in sports programs and other activities that allow them to interact with male adults.

It's no longer a cause for dismissal in the military for a woman to get pregnant, and there are supportive services for single parents. In addition, "the military does force you to live up to your parenting responsibilities," she says. She is required to maintain a list of short-term and long-term caregivers for her children, in case she should be deployed on short notice. "Luckily, I have never had to put these plans into action," Karen says.

Dad's Point of View

John is a divorced auto mechanic raising two boys, ages 9 and 14. He says he tries very hard to be both mom and dad, especially since the boys' mother is not involved in their life. Forced to work three jobs to make ends meet, he worries because he is able to spend so little time with the boys. Over the summer, the 9-year-old will be in a day-care camp from 7:00 A.M. to 6:00 P.M.

John spends his spare time cooking, cleaning, shopping for food, and doing laundry. Because of his work situation—he works from 6:00 A.M. to 8:30 P.M. at his jobs, and then for several hours at night after the boys are asleep—he doesn't have time to meet anyone new.

"I worry because the soft, feminine side of a parent is missing from their lives," he says. "I remember that was so important to me as a kid. I got that from my mother," he says. "I try, but I just don't think I'm as soft as a mother would be."

In an effort to balance the kinds of influence to which his sons are exposed, John asks his own mother to come over several times a week, and to babysit for the boys on other occasions.

For Reflection

It really does "take a village to raise a child." How many times in the past month did you find yourself trying to play both mom and dad?

Instead of fretting over the lack of two parents in your child's life, think about how you could improve your own responses as a mom or dad.

Children's needs are infinite. Can you handle the fact that some of your kids' needs may simply go unmet?

SET GOALS FOR YOURSELF

Setting goals can make it easier to find your way through the jungle of pressing responsibilities of home, work, and child care.

In More Depth

If you've ever tried to juggle three separate and equally difficult jobs, you know that it's imperative to have a plan and a goal if you're going to do anything other than spin your wheels.

It's so easy to get caught up in the day-to-day hassles that you forget to step back and look at the big picture—but this is exactly what you need to do from time to time. You wouldn't try to find your way through a big city without a map, and you shouldn't try to navigate through a complicated life without at least some idea of knowing where you're going, and what it will take to get there. Defining and fulfilling a goal are also important skills to teach your children; if they see you living your life according to a plan, chances are they will absorb the lesson themselves.

Knowing how to set goals and achieve them will also help you deal with negative emotions that often crop up when you're trying to handle the many responsibilities of a single working parent.

Mom's Point of View

Cheryl was a working mom with one 10-year-old daughter and a dream. While currently employed in an unexciting job as an office manager, Cheryl had always dreamed of becoming a teacher.

"I had my bachelor's degree in English, but I never really did anything with it," she says. "I always thought I would really love to teach."

The obstacles seemed insurmountable. College tuition was not cheap, and the nearest colleges would require her to retake many of the same undergrad courses, since she had been out of college for many years. Working all day and helping her ex-husband care for her daughter meant that she could take only one course at a time. Under that schedule, it would be years before she would be certified to teach—and then she was not sure she would be able to get a job. But the dream did not die.

Cheryl felt as if she were treading water at her job. She was going nowhere and was unable to spend summers with her daughter. After several years of unhappiness, she finally began the admissions process to graduate school. She's now halfway through the course program and thrilled to be making progress toward a goal.

"I just felt so aimless," she says. "Now I feel like I'm on track and accomplishing something. It's made all the difference in my outlook and in how I feel about my present job, and I'm thrilled that I'll be able to stay home with my daughter more often."

Dad's Point of View

Sometimes life seemed almost impossible to Nick, who was the sole custodial parent of two active boys and whose ex-wife was not interested in helping out. Admitting that there were days when he just felt like "running away," Nick says what helped him get through the first 2 years was his realization that he needed to be focused on a goal.

"If you're not focused, you'll get lost," Nick says. "I realized I needed a goal. You need to set up some plans so that you understand you're working not just for yourself, but for the whole family. You need to live more than just minute to minute." Nick focused on building a house on their lot to replace their old trailer, a project that took almost a year to complete.

For Reflection

Do you know what you want to be doing in the next 5 years?

Make a list of five things you'd like to do that you don't think you have the time, money, or training to accomplish. Brainstorm ways that you might accomplish these goals.

If you hesitate to set goals for yourself, could it be because you're afraid you might not reach them?

TAKE 30 MINUTES A DAY...

Spending just 30 minutes a day interacting with your kids on their level can reap big benefits.

In More Depth

It's certainly not easy for any working parents to discover 30 unused minutes a day when they're not working, cleaning the carpet, washing the dog, catching up on bills, and so on. But that's exactly why psychiatrist Stanley Greenspan believes it's so important; otherwise, we might not find the time to interact. In his book *Playground Politics: Understanding the Emotional Life of Your School Age Child,* Dr. Greenspan suggests you spend 30 minutes a day doing something that your child initiates. For preschoolers, he recommends you get right down on the floor and interact. With school-age children, you could take a walk or lie on the bed and chat about whatever is on their minds.

The key is to build up a warm, trusting relationship on your child's terms. Sound easy? Not for lots of us, Dr. Greenspan says. Our busy schedules seem to get in the way of spending time with our kids. Whatever it takes—turning off the TV, postponing dinner for a half-hour, taking a quicker bath—we need to spend a bit of time each day in uninterrupted conversation with our children.

While you're playing or interacting with your kids during this time, don't try to take control—don't dictate what or how you'll play, or what your children should tell you. Sit back and let the kids take over.

Mom's Point of View

Jean Marie is a busy single mom who teaches anthropology at a nearby university. She found it a real challenge to continue in her career while parenting her 4-year-old son Jess. There never seemed to be enough time to do everything.

"One of the best pieces of advice I ever read is that when you first come in the door after working all day, don't try to start dinner or clean up the house," she says. "Instead, spend the first half-hour totally focused on your children, and let them take the lead in doing whatever they want to do. They need to feel they are the center of your universe more than they need to eat dinner on time!"

Dad's Point of View

By the time Mike got home after an exhausting hour-long fight with city traffic, all he wanted was to stretch out on the couch and sleep. Instead, he felt as if he had to run around and clean up, get dinner on the table, listen to homework, and then get his two sons, ages 10 and 6, into bed.

"My life was just one chore after another," he says, with little time for enjoying either of his boys. He'd had a hard time since his divorce and felt it was taking all his resources just to keep working and maintain some semblance of order at home. "The responsibility is an incredible load, and it never stops," he says.

Then the older boy got in trouble at school, and the younger one began acting out with temper tantrums at day care. It was obvious that stress was taking its toll.

Mike talked about his situation with the day-care director, who was sympathetic toward his plight. "She pointed out that while I was always busy dong things *for* the boys' welfare, I wasn't really doing things *with* them. They needed more of my time."

Assured that he didn't have to spend hours every day playing with his sons in order to make a difference, Mike began slowly the very next day. "When I came home, I went up to my sons' bedroom, where they were playing with the computer. I sat down with them and asked them to show me some of the games." To Mike's astonishment, the boys were thrilled at his interest.

He also made plans to spend one morning a weekend with one of his sons, leaving the other son with his mother for a few hours. Each boy alternated "his" weekend morning, when they might eat breakfast at a fast-food restaurant, go fishing at a local pond, or take a walk through the park.

"Once I realized that the most important thing to do for my boys was to give them some of my time, the whole situation improved dramatically," Mike says.

For Reflection

When was the last time that you got down and played with your child without reading a magazine during a checkers game or watching TV while you were supposed to be playing with Barbies?

If someone asked your child whether or how often you play with her or him, what would your child say?

In what ways could you include your child during errands in order to bring the two of you closer?

FIND A FRIEND

Former friends often fade away after a divorce. Make a real effort to find new friends who can share the joy and sorrow of your new life.

In More Depth

Sadly, one of the big problems that many single working parents report is that when the divorce becomes public knowledge, former friends drift away. Some may be uncomfortable around you as a singleton because they knew you as a couple. Others may feel that their loyalty is divided—or that it lies with your ex. Still others may find your new freedom a threat.

At the same time, divorced parents report, single friends without children think they don't have much in common with you. And often, friends at work don't want to hear about your problems, your divorce, or your anxiety. You're there to do a job and that's all anybody really expects.

When you spend all day at work in a stressful environment, it can be especially difficult to come home at night and not be able to talk out your fears and frustrations with an adult partner. This is why it's crucial to find friends who can share your feelings and experience.

Some parents find support groups to be helpful. Others join church or political groups or interest organizations in search of like-minded souls. Whatever you choose, realize that as much as you love your children, there are some things you shouldn't really be discussing with them. You need an *adult* friend to blow off steam and discuss options in order to help you carry the load of job, family, and home.

Mom's Point of View

Arlene works at home and spends almost all her free time with her daughter, 9, and son, 12. It's been this way for quite some time, ever since her divorce, when she quit her public relations job to stay at home and work for herself. While she loves the independence, she misses her work friends and the interaction of adults, including her ex-husband.

"Whole days would go by and the only contact I'd have outside of my family was with the mail carrier or the express delivery truck," she says. "It didn't bother me at first, but after a while I realized I missed going out to lunch, sitting around discussing the latest movie or hot TV show." She realized that most of her friends had been those she'd known at work, so it was logical to assume that this was the best place she should look.

"Since we live in a rural area, I didn't know too many other women who were PR consultants," she says. Instead, she joined a local professional women's group, a group for writers, and the board of her local library. Instantly, she found herself surrounded by people with similar interests. "I couldn't believe how easy it was, once I went to the places where like-minded women congregate," she says.

Dad's Point of View

Harry is coowner of a motorcycle shop and divorced father of a hyperactive 8-year-old son who needs daily medication to balance his behavior. Despite the fact that his wife had grown tired of being married and wanted her freedom, abandoning her son with little remorse, Harry was upset to find that most of the couple's friends turned their backs on him.

"I wasn't the one who left," he says, "and I wasn't the one who refused to go to counseling." But when his wife walked out, doors closed to him. "My friends from my single days who were still single had really different interests," he said. He didn't really have any friends who were divorced, and night after night he came home alone to an empty apartment.

Eventually, his cousin invited him to a meeting for single parents, held at a local church. When Harry walked in, he suddenly realized what he'd been missing for the past months.

"At last, I was able to talk about things with other people who knew what I was going through," he says. "I couldn't really talk about this stuff at work, and nobody else wanted to listen." He was so thrilled with finding some kindred spirits that he made plans to go out for coffee after the meeting and continue the conversations. He's been meeting with the group twice a month since then, and has found that the experience made a big difference in his life.

"I'm not so depressed now, and there's an outward focus in my life. I'm not looking inward all the time and worrying."

For Reflection

Your kids see their friends all the time. When was the last time you saw a friend socially?

Think back over the past 5 years. How many new friends have you made? How many old friends have you lost contact with?

Make a list of 10 places you could go to meet new friends. Think of ways to suggest getting together and doing something socially.

BUILD A SUPPORT NETWORK

Trying to do it all alone can feel like a Herculean task. There's no need—find a support network and lean a little.

In More Depth

Parenthood was meant to be a partnership. When that's just not feasible, custodial parents who cope with running a home, making a living, and taking care of the children may find themselves in way over their heads. If the child's other parent simply won't help, you may need to find a safety net to fall back on when times get rough. It's time to build your own network. All parents can use such help, but single working parents have a real need for that second opinion: other people who can offer advice or help—or just another way of looking at a problem.

Can you imagine how much of a relief it is to realize you don't need to know everything? You can find support all around you: Community parenting classes and single-parent organizations such as Parents Without Partners are good places to start. Keep your ears open, and you may hear of a neighbor who's willing to help with transportation or child care in exchange for a favor from you.

Mom's Point of View

Life since her divorce had been tough for Sharon, who retained custody of her two daughters, ages 3 and 6. Unable to extract the court-ordered support payments for the children's care, Sharon struggled to make ends meet and find the time to spend with the girls she adored.

It was at her pediatrician's office that she first saw the notice for "Mom's Day Out." Normally she avoided formal get-togethers, but this day she was feeling at the end of her rope. The baby had an ear infection and the antibiotics to treat the condition were expensive. Both girls were fussy and demanding, and Sharon was exhausted from being up all night.

What Sharon liked about the notice was that kids were part of the group. The moms were all working parents, so they got together on Saturdays at each other's houses. The kids played together in another room, and the women were able to relax, share war stories, and connect with other adults.

"It was the best thing I ever did," she says today. "My girls liked playing at the others' houses, and I found that the chance to relax with other divorced women with kids was wonderful."

Dad's Point of View

Bob loved his son more than anything else in the world, and he desperately wanted to protect him from some of his own unfortunate mistakes. But whenever his son got into trouble, Bob would panic. "I just didn't know what I was doing wrong as a parent. I was investing all my time in my son—I didn't have a life of my own—but it didn't seem to be enough." Bob also worried that his son wasn't getting enough of a woman's influence—what he calls the "soft, gentle stuff."

At the same time, he was upset because he had no time for himself. The relentless pressure to make sure someone was there to watch over his son was unbearable sometimes. "I'm ashamed of the way I feel," he said, "but sometimes I just want to crawl in bed and pull the covers over my head."

When a neighbor recommended a community parenting workshop, Bob eagerly signed up. Not only did he come away with a fresh perspective, but he was able to meet some other parents in his situation. Together they set up their own group meeting at each other's houses twice a month.

"It may sound crazy, but just meeting some other parents in my situation helped a lot," Bob says. "Now I know that when things get rough, I can call someone else who's been there. We can talk, and at least I don't feel so alone."

For Reflection

Who can you call on when you need help—do you have your own support network?

Make a list of five things you could do to try to build your own support network independent of family members.

Do you feel that you should be able to do it all, without seeking outside help? Does this make your life easier or more difficult?

About the Author

Carol A. Turkington has written twelve other books, including *Reflections for Working Women* (McGraw-Hill). She is also a frequent contributor to *Self, Vogue, The New York Times* syndicate, and many other publications.